QUANTUM LEARNING

QUANTUM LEARNING

UNLEASH THE GENIUS WITHIN YOU

BOBBI DePORTER
with MIKE HERNACKI

PIATKUS

Permissions

Excerpt from *Creative Growth Games* by Eugene Raudsepp reprinted by permission of The Putnam Publishing Group from *Creative Growth Games* by Eugene Raudsepp. Copyright © 1977 by Eugene Raudsepp.

"The Nature of Water: Commonplace but Unique," by Tom L. McKnight, *Physical Geography: A Landscape Appreciation*, 3rd ed. ©1990, pp. 229–231. Reprinted by permission of Prentice Hall, Englewood Cliffs, New Jersey.

"Education's Ecstasy Explosion," by Lyelle Palmer. Reprinted in part with permission from *Holistic Education Review*, 39 Pearl Street, Brandon, Vermont 05733-1007.

"Making Friends with Mountain Gorillas," by Dian Fossey. Reprinted in part from *National Geographic* magazine, January, 1970 issue by permission of the National Geographic Society, Washington, D.C.

Mind Mapping™ is a registered trademark of Tony Buzan. Used with permission from Tony Buzan, Buzan Centre of Palm Beach, 415 Federal Hwy, Lake Park, Florida 33403

© 1992 by Bobbi DePorter

First published in Great Britain in 1993
by Judy Piatkus (Publishers) Ltd of
5 Windmill Street, London W1P 1HF

**The moral right of the author
has been asserted**

*A catalogue record for this book is
available from the British Library*

ISBN 0–7499–1213–8

Designed by Linus Saint James
Illustrations by Ellen Duris
Photography by Jill Fineberg and Mark Reardon

Printed and bound in Great Britain by
Bookcraft Ltd, Midsomer Norton, Avon

Acknowledgments

Collaborating with Mike Hernacki has been an enjoyable and illuminating process. I appreciate his support and I've learned a lot from him. His tenacity made this book a reality.

This book came together because of a very special team of people. Thank you to Denise Brown, with whom I work at Learning Forum, who took thoughts, notes, and research, and created flow and form. And to Vicki Townsend Gibbs, who continued the process by adding her input and professionalism.

I have much appreciation for Linus Saint James for his many long hours at the Macintosh creating graphic visual representations, along with the text, making it possible to be consistent with the way we present material at SuperCamp. Thank you to Ellen Duris for her illustrations and helpful advice.

Thank you to all who assisted at the Learning Forum office: Kim Bledsoe for her proofreading, Tricia Huppert for her Mind Maps, and others for their ideas, comments, and general support — Mark Reardon, Michael Kaufman, Cathy Essa, Shelby Reeder, Beth Quinette, Leslie Mendoza, Pam Farnum, Stan Adams, Barry Dworak, Mark Ogle, Renee Switzer, and Rob Dunton.

To my literary agent, Sandra Dijkstra, who first suggested the idea for the book, and to Trish Todd at Dell Publishing, I extend my thanks for their support and guidance.

I thank my publicist, Andrea Nordstrom Caughey, for her assistance and enthusiasm. Thanks also to Steve Curtis for his friendship and marketing advice over the years, and to Don DePorter, Robert and Kim Kiyosaki, D.C. Cordova, Bill Galt, David Neenan, Lynn Dhority, Paula Feldman, and Jim Marino for their ongoing support.

The Quantum Learning methods used at SuperCamp were developed over ten years, with input from many people. Thank you to the staff of the first SuperCamp, who believed, and contributed to creating the adventure, and to all who have shared the vision over the years, for their ideas and innovations.

I especially want to thank Greg Simmons, Linda Brown-Schaeff, John Le Tellier, Dan Mikels, Kate Neale, Rich Allen, Michael Carr, Steve Snyder, Joelle James, Maggie Weiss, Andrew Bisaha, Jane Gibson, Jan Hensley, David Lindquist, Diane Hamilton, Marilyn Perona, Doug McPhee, Jeanette Vos-Groenendal, Kathy Carroll, Brian Blackstock, Kim Zoller, Julie McNamara, Scott Bornstein, Julie and Skip Domville, Toni Bowen, Rolf and Ann Nevin-Parta, Beryel Dorscht, Tamara Drean, Annette Segal, Kathy Forman-Hitt, Lee Pliscou, Monica Bouten, Richard Hollicky, Rob Abernathy, Vicki Peterson, Leigh Akins, Susan Adams, Cindy Pook, Tia Robinson, Paula Mantel, Barbara Lindquist, Tom Pew, Gayle Copeland, Rick Meyers, Connie Messina, Jan Storrs, the staff of On The Edge, and so many others.

For brilliance in the creation of programs, I acknowledge Eric Jensen, my cofounder and business partner for the first five years of SuperCamp, and Marshall Thurber, my partner and cofounder of the Burklyn Business School.

To my husband, Joe Chapon, who is both my business and life partner, much love and appreciation for his constant encouragement and support in my own personal growth and for the joy of sharing together the development of SuperCamp.

I dedicate this book to my son, Grant, and daughter, Dana, and to all who have participated in and contributed to SuperCamp.

— B.D.

Contents

Introduction

My Challenge and Yours

Flip through the pages of this book and you'll notice it's a lot different from other books. The left-hand pages are filled with lines of ordinary type, while most of the right-hand pages contain drawings, diagrams, symbols — just about anything *but* lines of ordinary type.

Look a bit more closely and you'll find special pages at the beginning and end of most chapters. The chapters start with a quick rundown of the benefits you can expect from the material, and end with a checklist so you can verify what you learned. As you read, you'll see that I repeat material, often restating it in different ways, in a different type style, or in graphic form.

I use these and other techniques because they're in tune with how your brain works, with the ways you learn best. The techniques have been tested and measured for years. They work. Quantum Learning works. Thousands of Quantum Learners whom we've trained over the years will attest to that fact. In this book, my challenge is to prove to you that it works. I've taken on this challenge eagerly.

But I'm also challenging *you*. To read this book with an open mind. To set aside your notions about how a book should look or what it should say. To suspend judgment about how much and how fast you can learn. To surprise yourself with your own ability. And to have fun every step of the way.

— Bobbi DePorter
Oceanside, California

1

Relearning How
to Learn

Imagine a business school with a curriculum so powerful
that students emerge after only six weeks saying things
like, "It gave me more ammunition than four years of
college!" and, "I now know I can learn anything! To say
my intelligence has expanded ten times would not be an
exaggeration." A school where business people not only
learn a great deal about theory and practice, they also
build their self-confidence, feel more successful in their
lives, and have fun — all at the same time. A business
school that strengthens the body and nurtures the soul
while educating the mind.

There was such a place — the Burklyn Business School,
which I cofounded in the late 1970s. Burklyn taught conventional subjects, such as marketing, negotiation, and
accounting, but in an unconventional way. While all the
well-known business schools were turning out specialized
professional managers for major corporations, Burklyn
was producing entrepreneurs who learned a lot about
themselves as well as business.

We began with the premise that an entrepreneur needs
a thorough understanding of business as a whole, not just
one highly specialized area. So we approached the subjects
we taught as entire experiences, rather than "material"
to be digested and regurgitated. We also made the learning experience applicable to real life, rather than purely
academic or theoretical.

Whether we're enrolled in school, or are just "students of life," the most valuable thing to learn is *how to learn.* For this reason, the first week of Burklyn's six-week curriculum was spent on basic learning skills such as notetaking, memory, and speed reading. At the same time, the school sought to create an atmosphere of safety and trust among students and instructors. The combination of these factors, plus the focus on the whole brain, enabled students to study more effectively and absorb and recall an awesome amount of technical material. The school also turned out to be quite successful at producing joyous, confident, lifelong learners.

Most Burklyn students remembered that their primary or secondary school experiences weren't anything like this. They made important discoveries about themselves as learners, realizing for the first time that they actually loved learning, even though some had spent twelve or sixteen or twenty years hating school. The experience also changed their lives in ways none of us had anticipated. Many Burklyn graduates gave up secure jobs in large corporations and went into partnerships. Many altered the way they did business, going from win/lose to win/win in orientation.

More and more often we heard comments like, "My child would benefit from a school like this," and "If my kids had this much fun learning, they'd get all A's." I began to see the tremendous need there was (and is) for a love of learning to be nurtured in a student's early years. And so, along with some highly talented and dedicated people, I began developing SuperCamp in the early 1980s. It was at SuperCamp that the principles and methods of Quantum Learning took shape.

The Miracle of SuperCamp

In 1981, Eric Jensen, Greg Simmons, and I began adapting what had been learned at Burklyn into the first program for teenagers. We started by talking with almost two hundred parents about what kids needed the most. Then we went to work creating a ten-day program that would combine confidence-building, learning skills, and communication skills in an environment of fun.

When the program got under way we began to see some amazing breakthroughs that told us we were definitely heading in the right direction. Ultimately, it was more successful than we ever expected, and became a significant event in the lives of the teenagers who attended.

At SuperCamp, the curriculum is a precisely orchestrated combination of three elements: academic skills, physical achievements, and life skills. Underlying this curriculum is a basic philosophy. We believe that to be effective, learning can and *must* be fun. Learning is a lifelong proposition people *can* undertake joyfully and successfully. We believe that the *whole person* is important — the intellectual, the physical, and the emotional/personal — and that high self-esteem is an essential ingredient in the make-up of healthy, happy learners.

To support this philosophy we take care in setting up the environment so that students feel important, safe and comfortable. The physical environment is made attractive with plants, art and music. The instructors pay attention to the emotional environment by building up rapport and establishing emotional safety zones with students before exposing them to challenges at which they can realistically succeed.

Today, thousands of children and young people are graduates of SuperCamp. Many of them have gone on to college and to successful careers in every imaginable field. In their letters to us, a gratifying number of them trace their first real successes to their experience at camp.

Camps are held throughout the United States and around the world, in places such as Singapore and Moscow. This incredible growth has occurred mostly through word-of-mouth. Why? *Because it works*. Students can arrive reluctant and apprehensive, yet leave feeling that they've just spent the best ten days of their entire lives.

Quantum Learning

The company that produces SuperCamp is called Learning Forum. We think of our approach as *Quantum Learning* — a body of learning methods and philosophies that have proven to be effective in school and in business . . . for all types of people, and for all ages.

Quantum Learning has its roots in the work of Dr. Georgi Lozanov, a Bulgarian educator who experimented with what he calls "suggestology" or "suggestopedia." His premise is that *suggestion* can and does affect the outcome of the learning situation, and every single detail provides either positive or negative suggestion. Some of the techniques he uses to provide positive suggestion are seating students comfortably, using background music in the classroom, increasing individual participation, using posters to suggest greatness while reinforcing information, and having a teacher well-trained in the art of suggestive instruction.

Another term used almost interchangeably with suggestology is "accelerated learning." Accelerated learning is defined as "enabling the student to learn with impressive speed, little conscious effort, and a great deal of pleasure." It brings together elements that at first glance don't appear to have a lot in common: fun, games, colours, positive thinking, physical fitness, and emotional health. But all these elements work together to produce an effective learning experience.

Quantum Learning includes important aspects of neurolinguistic programming (NLP), which is the study of how the brain organizes information. It probes the relationship between language and behaviour and can be used to create rapport between students and teachers. Educators with knowledge of NLP know how to use positive languaging to promote positive actions — an important factor for stimulating the most effective brain functioning. They also can pinpoint and make the most of each individual's best learning style, and create "anchors" out of successful, confident moments.

Quantum Learning is a body of learning methods and philosophies proven effective for all ages.

Environment

Atmosphere
- Positive
- Safe, supportive
- Relaxed
- Exploratory
- Joyous

Physical
- Movement
- Breaks
- State changes
- Games
- Physiology
- Hands-on
- Participation

Surroundings
- Comfortable
- Well lit
- Visually exciting
- Musical

Values and Beliefs

Resources

Interaction
- Knowledge
- Experience
- Connections
- Inspiration

Methods
- Modeling
- Games
- Simulations
- Metaphor

Learning To Learn Skills
- Memory
- Reading
- Writing
- Note-taking
- Creativity
- Learning Styles
- Communication
- Relationships

We define Quantum Learning as "interactions that transform energy into radiance." All life is energy. A well-known formula in quantum physics is *Matter* times the *Speed of Light Squared* equals *Energy*. You may have seen this expressed as $E = mc^2$.

Our physical bodies are matter. As learners, it is our purpose to experience as much light as possible: interactions, connections, inspirations — so as to produce radiant energy.

Quantum Learning incorporates suggestology, accelerated learning techniques, and NLP with our own theories, beliefs, and methods. It includes key concepts from many other learning theories and strategies including:

- Right/left brain theory
- The triune brain theory
- Modality preference (visual, auditory, kinesthetic)
- Theory of multiple intelligences
- Holistic education
- Experiential learning
- Metaphoric learning
- Simulation/gaming

If any of these terms throw you, relax. They'll be explained in upcoming chapters.

Jeannette Vos-Groenendal, a SuperCamp instructor, wrote her doctoral dissertation on the results of Super-Camp. She says that, based on data collected during the 1983–1989 years, the SuperCamp program "has been found to be very successful and should be considered as a model for replication." The diagram opposite shows the major benefits derived by students.

She also points out that the program "has found a way to meet the different abilities of students." And she feels the methods could be used to lower the drop-out rate in schools nationwide.

Research shows that SuperCamp "has been found to be very successful and should be considered as a model for replication."

— Jeannette Vos-Groenendal
1991, doctoral dissertation

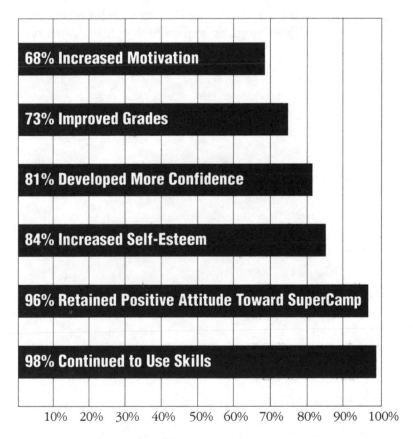

68% Increased Motivation

73% Improved Grades

81% Developed More Confidence

84% Increased Self-Esteem

96% Retained Positive Attitude Toward SuperCamp

98% Continued to Use Skills

10% 20% 30% 40% 50% 60% 70% 80% 90% 100%

This study involved 6,042 SuperCamp graduates, ages 12–22, and utilized quantitative and qualitative data.

The most important point to remember now is that the material in this book has been tested and proven effective by over ten years of real, live experience. Very little is theoretical. It's all stuff that has worked, again and again, for people of every type. And the best of it has been distilled into these pages. When you've read this book, you'll not only be a better learner, you'll also be a more efficient, more eager, more excited learner. You'll be able to use the principles of Quantum Learning to get another degree, or another job, or just become better at your present job. Most important, you'll have fun along the way. So let's get on to the most incredible learning experience you'll ever have!

2

The Limitless Power
of Your Mind

Did you know . . .

 your brain has the same potential as Albert Einstein's?

 there is physical, scientific evidence proving the adage about your brain, Use it or lose it?

We are all born with an insatiable curiosity. And we all possess the tools we need to satisfy it. Have you ever watched a baby explore a new toy? He puts it in his mouth to see what it tastes like. He shakes it, holds it up, and slowly moves it around so he can see how each side catches the light. He sticks it in his ear, drops it on the ground and picks it up again, takes it apart, and inspects it piece by piece.

This exploratory process has recently been called "global learning." Global learning is such an effective and natural way for a human being to learn that the mind of a child up to age six or seven is a veritable sponge, absorbing facts, physical properties, and linguistic intricacies in a completely joyful and stress-free manner. Add to this process the factors of positive feedback and environmental stimulation, and you've created the perfect conditions for unlimited learning.

Let's look at some of the learning milestones in the early life of a normal, healthy child. Chances are this child is very much like you were. By the time you reached your first birthday, you had probably taught yourself to walk — a process so complicated physically and neurologically that it's almost impossible to explain in words or teach without demonstrating. Yet you were able to do this in spite of countless falls and bumps, and you never felt like a failure when you stumbled. Why is this? I'm sure that as an adult, you can think of several cases when you've given up learning something new after failing only once or twice. So why did you try again and again when you were learning to walk?

The answer is, you had *no concept of failure.* To help matters, your parents were convinced you would learn it if you kept trying, and they were always there to encourage you. Every success was met with rejoicing and celebration, which pumped you up for even more success.

By the time you were about two years old, you had begun to communicate in language, a skill you learned without grammar books, classes, or tests. In fact, if

You accomplished remarkable feats in your early years, thanks to the incredible power of your mind.

1st Year —   Learned to walk.

2nd Year —   Began to communicate in language.

5th Year —   Knew 90 percent of all words regularly used by adults.

6th Year —   Learned to read.

you're like most people, before your fifth birthday you learned about 90 percent of all the words you'll use regularly during your lifetime. And if you grew up in a home where more than one language was spoken, you probably were fluent in both of them.

At age six or seven, you tackled what educators agree is the hardest learning task a human being can undertake — you learned how to read. You did all this thanks to the tremendous power of your own brain.

Then one day, probably in first or second grade, you were sitting in class and the teacher said, "Who knows the answer to this question?" You raised your hand, bouncing on the edge of your seat with excitement until the teacher called your name. With confidence you called out the answer. Then you heard some of the other kids laughing and the teacher saying, "No, that's wrong. I'm surprised at you!"

You were embarrassed in front of your friends and the teacher, who was one of the most important authority figures in your life at the time. Your confidence was shaken, and a seed of self-doubt implanted itself in your psyche.

For many people, that's the beginning of a negative self-image. From that point on, learning becomes a chore. Self-doubt grows inside you, and you begin to take fewer and fewer risks.

In 1982, Jack Canfield, an expert on self-esteem, reported the results of a study in which one hundred children were assigned to a researcher for a day. The job of the researcher was to record how many negative and positive comments the child received throughout the course of the day. Canfield's findings were that on average, each child received 460 negative or critical comments, and only 75 positive or supportive comments. That's over six times more negative than positive strokes!

This continuous negative feedback is deadly. After a few years of school, an actual "learning shutdown"

Children, on the average, receive 460 negative or critical comments and 75 positive or supportive comments every day!

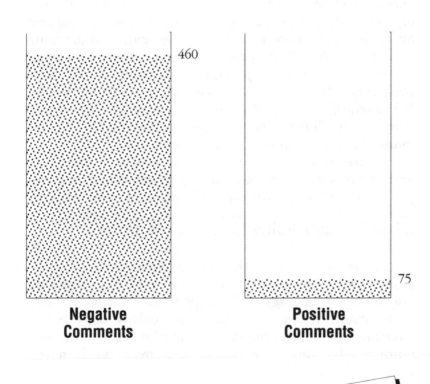

460

Negative Comments

75

Positive Comments

What would happen if children received all positive or supportive comments?

occurs, and children block their learning experiences involuntarily. By the end of elementary school, the very word *learning* can make a lot of students feel tense and overwhelmed.

At about the same age that this learning shutdown is happening, traditional school switches from a fun, holistic, "global learning" approach to one that is rigid, linear, and language-oriented. Suddenly, teachers expect students to sit still for an hour at a time, at rows of desks facing forward. The teacher stands and lectures about a given subject. Gone are the games and group activities, colorful art projects, homey touches, and all the other "frivolous" aspects of elementary school. As it progresses, the education process changes from the global learning of early childhood to a system that is predominantly left-brained. This "unbalancing" leaves many students feeling uninspired and unworthy.

Before going on, let's take a brief course on the brain and see how a switch back to whole-brain learning can get you on track to learning with ease and enjoyment.

A Lay Person's Guide to the Human Brain

The human brain is the most complex mass of protoplasm known to exist in this universe. It is the only known organ so highly developed that it can literally study itself. When nurtured by a healthy body and a stimulating environment, a functioning brain can remain active and reactive for well over one hundred years.

Your brain has three basic parts: the stem or "reptile brain," the limbic system or "mammalian brain," and the neocortex. Researcher Dr. Paul MacLean has termed it the "triune brain" because of the three parts, each of which developed during a different time in our evolutionary history. Each part also has a distinct neurostructure and set of tasks to perform.

First in evolutionary development was the stem or reptile brain. We share this element with all reptiles; it

Your brain has three basic parts, which together are known as the "triune brain."

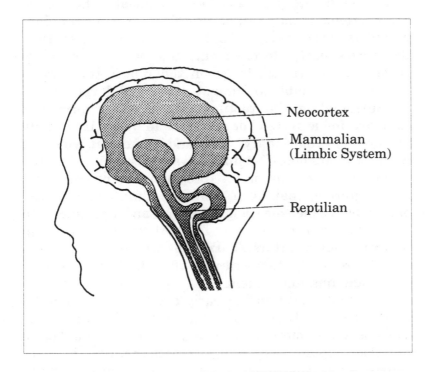

Neocortex

Mammalian
(Limbic System)

Reptilian

is the lowest intelligence component of the human species. This part of the brain is in charge of sensory motor functions — knowledge of physical reality that comes from our five senses.

Behavior that's seated in the reptile brain is related to the survival instinct, the drive to promote the species. Its concerns are food, shelter, reproduction, and protection of territory. When you feel unsafe, the reptile brain prompts you to stand and fight or run from danger. This is the so-called "fight or flight" response. During man's early development, this was a necessary response. Unfortunately, when the reptile brain dominates, we're unable to think at a very high level.

Surrounding the reptile brain is the enormously complex limbic system, or mammalian brain. It is vastly "higher" in evolutionary terms and is the part we share with all mammals. The limbic system is situated in the middle part of your brain. Its functions are emotional and cognitive; that is, it contains your feelings, your experience of pleasure, your memory, and your ability to learn. It also controls your biorhythms, such as sleep patterns, hunger, thirst, blood pressure, heart rate, sexual desire, body temperature and chemistry, metabolism, and immune system.

The limbic system is clearly a vital part of human preservation. (The fact that the part of the brain that controls your emotions also controls all of your bodily functions explains why your emotions can directly affect your health.) The limbic system is your central control panel, using as its input the information from your senses of sight, sound, bodily sensation, and less often, taste and smell. It then distributes the information to the thinking part of your brain, which is the neocortex.

The neocortex wraps around the top and sides of the limbic system, making up 80 percent of your total brain matter. This part of your brain is the seat of your intellect. It sorts out the messages received through your vision, hearing, and bodily sensations. Processes that

Each part of your brain is responsible for different functions.

1. **Stem or reptile brain —**
   - Sensory Motor Functions
   - Survival
   - "Fight or Flight"

2. **Limbic system or mammalian brain —**
   - Feelings/Emotions
   - Memory
   - Biorhythms
   - Immune System

3. **Neocortex or thinking brain —**
   - Cerebral Thinking
   - Reasoning
   - Purposeful Behavior
   - Language
   - Higher Intelligences

come out of this sorting are reasoning, cerebral thinking, decision-making, purposeful behavior, language, voluntary motor control, and nonverbal ideation.

In the neocortex are all of the higher intelligences that make human beings unique as a species. Psychologist Dr. Howard Gardner has identified many specific intelligences or "ways of knowing" that may be developed within a human being. Among these intelligences are linguistic, mathematical, visual/spatial, kinesthetic/tactical, musical, interpersonal, and intra-personal.

Probably the highest of the intelligences — and the greatest form of creative thought — is *intuition*. Intuition is the ability to receive or perceive information that is not available to our five senses. This ability is extremely acute in children between the ages of four and seven. Too often, it's suppressed and crushed by authority figures who view it as irrational behavior. People are afraid of intuition because they think it somehow precludes rational thought. The truth is, intuition is based on rational thought and could not work without it!

How and When Intelligences Develop

All of the higher intelligences, including intuition, are present in the brain at birth, and over the first seven years of life they can unfold if properly nurtured.

For these intelligences to be properly nurtured, several conditions must be met:

- the lower neurostructures must be sufficiently developed to allow energy to move to a higher level;
- the child must feel physically and emotionally safe; and
- there must be a model to provide the appropriate stimulus.

Let's look at the timing of these developing intel-

Many higher intelligences, or "ways of knowing," have been identified.

- Linguisitic

- Mathematical

- Visual/Spatial

- Kinesthetic/Tactical

- Musical

- Interpersonal

- Intrapersonal

- Intuition

ligences. Linguistic ability unfolds while a person is still in the womb. A child isn't *taught* its native language; if the mother has the ability to speak, she can't prevent a child from learning it. In fact, if a child is exposed to language at any time during the first seven years, the linguistic intelligence will be activated.

In the first year of life, the sensory motor functions get going. This is accomplished through direct contact by the infant with its environment, by continual interactions with its mother and the things in its immediate world. When baby puts something in its mouth, holds it up to the light, and bangs it against another item, it is learning about that item in the only way available at this point — through the senses.

By age one or two, the sensory motor brain is sufficiently advanced, and the child shifts up to the next level of development. There is a terrific increase in neuron connections, and as the emotional-cognitive system fires up, the baby's behavior changes almost overnight. This new behavior is commonly known as the "terrible twos" and is dreaded by parents the world over. But consider this: It is absolutely essential that a child go through this emotional development in order to get to the higher thinking of the neocortex.

At this point, in addition to developing emotionally, the child is preparing for higher intellectual development through *play*. Imitation, storytelling, and other imaginative play-type activities are the ways children develop the metaphoric and symbolic abilities upon which all higher education rests.

By age four, the sensory motor and emotional cognitive neurostructures are 80 percent developed. Then and only then can nature afford the energy to move into the higher thinking modes. Now is when other intelligences open up for development. If properly nurtured, they will flourish. If the child feels threatened or if there is no model, these intelligences will eventually shut down by about age seven.

In the child who has been sufficiently nurtured,

By age four, the lower brain structures are 80 percent developed, and higher intelligences open up for development.

Sensory Motor Functions

Developed through direct contact with the environment.

Emotional-Cognitive System

Developed through play, imitation, and storytelling.

Higher Intelligences

Developed when properly nurtured and the child is emotionally healthy.

many of the higher thought processes can unfold and blossom joyfully and effortlessly. At this point, the sensory motor (reptile) brain is developed enough to operate on autopilot (subconsciously), kicking in only when it perceives danger. The limbic system is also highly developed and continues to monitor psychological safety and emotional health. When the child is emotionally healthy, he or she is free to operate in the higher realms of the neocortex.

The neocortex is made up of 12 to 15 billion nerve cells, called neurons. These cells are capable of interaction with other cells by vibration along branches, called dendrites. Each neuron is capable of interacting with neurons in its vicinity, which means there are more potential interactions between the cells in one human brain than there are atoms in the entire universe! These interactions also determine your ability to learn.

The key to the connection between dendrites is a substance called myelin. Without getting too technical, let me just explain that myelin is a fatty protein released by the brain to coat the connection between dendrites as new information is learned. This happens the first time a connection is made, and thereafter anytime there is proper stimulus from the environment to activate that connection again.

At the time of the first connection, it takes a lot of energy to "get" it. After that it gets easier and easier as the myelin forms a thicker coat. Eventually, with enough repetition, the connection becomes sufficiently "myelinated" and able to operate without effort while other connections are being made.

The process of myelination explains why it's so ineffective to present material in forty-five minute classes. According to internationally recognized author and learning researcher Joseph Pearce, the average child retains only about three percent of the information taught in this way.

Your brain has billions of nerve cells, called neurons, which are capable of interaction with other cells along branches called dendrites.

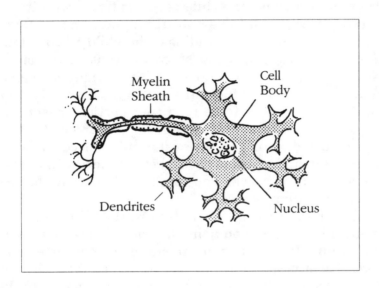

In order to get high retention, as either a child or an adult, a student needs total immersion in a subject. At SuperCamp, material is taught in intense, full-day classes. Typically, we see students reach the breakthrough "aha" stage sometime during the afternoon. That's the point at which they've become sufficiently myelinated to make the information part of their permanent brain structure.

Have you ever noticed that a child will often ask you to read a certain favorite story over and over again? Then after a while, the child seems satiated with it and is ready to move on to new stories. What's happening is, during the repeated rereadings, the child is absorbing the metaphoric and symbolic connections in the story. Neuron links are activated, and myelination begins. When the link is sufficiently myelinated, the child no longer has the need to be read that particular story all the time; once in a while is enough. After myelination has occurred, it needs reviewing only infrequently. If after years and years it hasn't been reviewed, the myelin begins to dissolve. You might call that the brain's way of "cleaning house."

Brain research scientist Dr. Marian Diamond has spent thirty years conducting a series of experiments on the brain. Her conclusion: At any age from birth until death, it is possible to increase your mental ability by environmental stimulation. Her life's work points to the fact that, where the brain is concerned, the old adage "Use it or lose it" is very good advice. The more your brain is stimulated by intellectual activity and interaction with the environment, the more connections it makes between cells. You can see that your potential is virtually limitless! (I'll discuss Dr. Diamond's research in more detail in Chapter 4, which concerns the learning environment.)

Right Brain, Left Brain

Your three-part brain is also divided into a right and

Through repetition, nerve cells become connected and myelinated to make easy recall of information. Without occasional review, myelin begins to dissolve.

Use it . . .

or

lose it

left hemisphere. These days, these two hemispheres are commonly known as the "right brain" and the "left brain." Experimentation with the two hemispheres has shown that each one is responsible for different modes of thinking, and each specializes in certain skills, although there is some crossover and interaction between the two sides.

The left-brain thinking processes are logical, sequential, linear, and rational. This side is highly organized. Though based in reality, it is capable of abstract and symbolic interpretation. Its modes of thinking lend themselves to the orderly tasks of verbal expression, writing, reading, auditory association, locating details and facts, phonetics, and symbolism.

The right-brain thinking modes are random, unordered, intuitive, and holistic. These modes are well suited for the nonverbal ways of knowing, such as feelings and emotions, haptic awareness (feeling the presence of objects or people), spatial awareness, shape and pattern recognition, music, art, color sensitivity, creativity, and visualization.

Both of the brain's hemispheres are of equal importance. People who favor both sides of the brain equally tend to be literally "in balance" in all aspects of their lives. Learning comes especially easy to them because they have the choice of calling upon whichever mode is needed most for the task at hand. Since most communication is expressed in verbal or written form, both of which are left-brain specialties, the fields of education, business, and science tend to be rather heavily weighted toward the left. In fact, if you're in the left-brain category, and you don't make a specific effort to include some right-brain activities in your life, the resultant unbalancing can cause you stress as well as poor mental and physical health.

To balance out society's tendency toward the left, it's important to include music and aesthetics in your learning experience and to give yourself positive feedback. All

Each of the two hemispheres of the brain is responsible for different modes of thinking and specializes in certain skills, although crossover does occur.

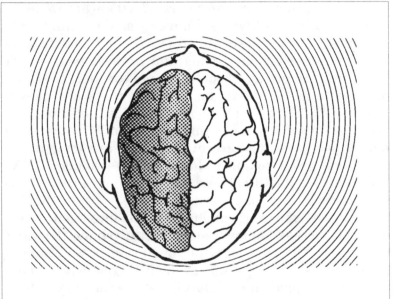

Left Brain
- Logical
- Sequential
- Linear
- Rational

Right Brain
- Random
- Unordered
- Intuitive
- Holistic

these things cause positive emotions, which make your brain more effective. Positive emotions lead to brain power, which leads to success, which leads to high self-esteem, which leads to positive emotions — a vigorous cycle spinning you higher and higher. (Have you ever noticed that very successful people seem to have an acute appreciation for the arts?)

Whether we're speaking about the limbic system or the neocortex, the right or left hemisphere, the point is that no single part of the brain works as fully or creatively on its own as it does when stimulated or supported by output from other parts. That's what we mean when we talk about whole-brain or global learning.

During the course of our lives, all of us come to some conclusions about our brains and brain power. Maybe your performance in school led you to conclude that your brain isn't as "good" as the brains of the students who consistently did better. Maybe you've decided that your brain is "good" at some things but not at others. Or maybe you've come to accept that there are some things you'll just never be able to learn because you don't have the brain for it. All of these conclusions are regrettable — and probably wrong.

Despite apparent differences in intelligence and level of success among people, we all share the same neurology. The physiology of your brain is very similar to that of any other person, even such famously brilliant thinkers as Einstein and Da Vinci. This means you have a tremendous opportunity. If you know of someone who exhibits the type of behavior you admire or who has achieved something you would like to accomplish, you can use that person as a *model*. And you can duplicate that person's success just by patterning your mind and body after his or hers. Behavioral scientists call this "modeling."

A classic case of modeling is the great British athlete Roger Bannister, the first person to run a mile in less than four minutes. Before he accomplished this feat,

Positive emotions lead to ever-increasing brain power, success, and self-esteem.

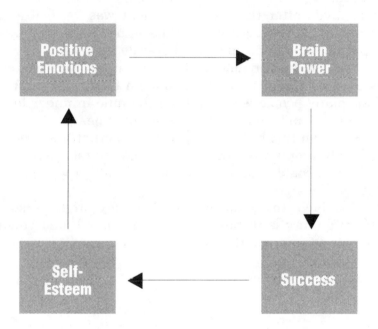

athletes — and sports doctors too — generally believed the four-minute mile was impossible for a human being to achieve. One doctor seriously argued that if a man ran that fast, his heart would burst from overexertion.

Obviously, Roger Bannister was not put off by this prediction. He just ran — faster than anyone in history. After thousands of athletes had trained for decades without breaking the four-minute barrier, Bannister did it, stunning the world with a time of 3 minutes, 59.4 seconds. Even after the accomplishment was verified and accepted, many said it was a fluke—that Bannister was superhuman and no one would ever do it again.

And yet, just one month later, his record was beaten by an Australian runner named John Landy. Soon after that, many people were running the mile in under four minutes — and steadily improving the time.

How can this be? One explanation is that there were suddenly people who could act as models, and then anybody who could copy them could accomplish what they did.

You have the same potential as any other person. The difference is in how you use your mind, and you'll see how as you read this book.

What one person can do, any other person has the potential to do.

Anthony Robbins, a peak performance strategist, author, and speaker, has helped hundreds of thousands of people to break through their limiting beliefs and unlock their giant potential. Tony's objective is to model the practices of peak performers, individuals who are consistently producing quality results. He discovers their core beliefs and uncovers the strategies that make them so effective. Then he teaches these beliefs and strategies to large groups of people.

One activity Tony teaches his students to model is firewalking, a process in which he leads barefoot participants across a bed of red-hot coals. He uses concepts of neurolinguistic programming (NLP) to help them accomplish this incredible feat. NLP, the study of how both verbal and nonverbal language affects our nervous system, was developed by John Grinder and Richard Bandler.

One of Tony's favorite examples of the power of modeling is Stu Mittleman, who broke a world's record by running 1,000 miles in just 11 days. Stu modeled the beliefs of a group of South American Indians who, as part of a celebration, run 75 miles a day just for fun.

By finding someone who has achieved what you desire, you save yourself not only energy, but a great deal of time. What would you like to do in your life? What obstacles would you like to overcome? Who do you want to be? Find someone who manifests your goal, then step in and duplicate his or her mental and physical behavior — and success will be yours.

3

The Power of WIIFM —
What's In It For Me?

Why should you read this chapter?

☑ Learn how to get yourself motivated to attain your goals.

☑ Know the steps to creating interest in anything.

☑ Discover what active learning is all about.

☑ Improve the quality of your life.

Before you do almost anything in your life, you either consciously or subconsciously ask yourself this very important question: "What's in it for me?" From the simplest daily task to the monumental life-changing decision, everything has to promise some personal benefit, or you have no motivation to do it.

For example, you wake up on Saturday morning and debate the benefits of going over to the health club to work out. Here's how your self-talk goes.

"Hmmm, I can stay here in this nice, comfy bed for another hour, or I can get myself up and dressed and go work out. Saturday's the only day of the week I can sleep in, and it's also the only day I have time to get any exercise. Well, there are lots of things I want to do today, and if I start off the day with a good workout, I'll feel energetic and look healthy. Okay, I'll get up."

If you hop out of bed at that moment, you've identified a benefit and taken action to secure it for yourself. But let's say that instead of hopping out of bed, you hesitate and your self-talk continues.

"On the other hand, working out will take two hours and sleeping in will use up only one hour, so by sleeping I'll have more time to get things done. Besides, this bed feels so-o-o good. Okay, I'll sleep in."

In this case, you identified a benefit in the second course of action that you found more appealing. Whether or not it makes sense, whether or not it's better for you, the more appealing alternative is the one you'll choose.

You also go through this process on a more profound level when you decide whether to make a job change, go back to school, ask for a raise, do a favor for a friend, attend a meeting, plant a vegetable garden, remodel your house, or anything else in which you must weigh benefit against effort or risk — or benefit against benefit.

Imagine you've just been offered a job in another state. When you ask, "What's in it for me?" you'll prob-

Everything you consider doing has to promise some personal benefit or you are unmotivated to do it.

Weighing benefits — the pluses and the minuses

ably consider salary, the possibility for advancement, housing costs in the new area, weather, the crime rate, quality of the schools, how far it is from relatives, whether there are adequate recreational facilities — and dozens of other factors. You'll weigh all of these against what you currently have *and* the effort it will take to make the move before you'll decide whether or not to accept the job.

We call the motivation you get from this mental exercise "WIIFM" (pronounced *wiffum*), an acronym for "What's in it for me?" And whether you're considering pumping iron, moving to a new state, or learning a new skill, you just aren't motivated to take action if the WIIFM doesn't outweigh the effort and risk involved — or if it doesn't outweigh the benefit of some other alternative.

Sometimes the WIIFM is very clear in your mind, and other times you have to look for it, or even invent it.

Creating Interest – A Powerful WIIFM for Learning

In many situations, finding WIIFM is synonymous with *creating interest* in what you're learning by linking it to the "real world." This is especially true in formal learning situations. Whether it's a night class, a weekend seminar, or a college course, you need to find a way to make it meaningful in your own life. Ask yourself, "How can I use this in my everyday life?"

Creating interest is easy for some subjects and harder for others, but you can almost always find something to interest you. Chances are you're already motivated to learn the information for some reason. Perhaps it will advance you in your career, or help you communicate better, or maybe it's a stepping-stone to higher education. If you've had a few years' experience in the job market, you also have a good sense of the real world and what it takes to get the most out of it, so it may be easier to create interest now than it was when you were younger.

Sometimes the WIIFM is very clear in your mind, and other times you have to look for it, or even invent it.

What's

In

It

For

Me

WIIFM is the
motivation received
from mentally
choosing between
the benefits and
costs of a decision.

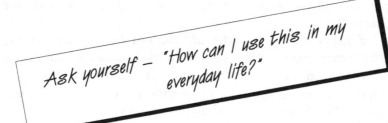

Ask yourself — *"How can I use this in my everyday life?"*

Let's say you've signed up for a Spanish class on Tuesday and Thursday evenings after work. You wanted to take this class or you wouldn't have signed up for it, but sometimes it's hard to stay motivated. After work, you have to rush to do the grocery shopping, eat dinner, go to the bank, and pick up your dry cleaning. What's more, after a long day on the job you're pretty tired and just want to relax in front of the television or read a book. How can you create the interest you need to continue going to class?

Where I live, it would be easy. In Southern California, a large part of the population is Spanish-speaking, so I come across the language as a part of my everyday life. I hear it as I walk down the aisles of the supermarket ("What are they saying? Are they talking about me?") and almost every other place I go. Plus, if I were to go to Mexico on vacation (which many people from this area do because it's a land rich in beauty, diversity, and cultural heritage — and because it's an easy drive), knowledge of Spanish would enable me to get around more freely and comfortably. Knowing the language would also help me find the best prices for lodging, figure out train and boat schedules, and ask directions to a bank, a telephone, or an ice machine. When sightseeing, it's also advantageous to talk to local people rather than depend solely on guidebooks for information.

Simply put, knowledge of Spanish would *enhance my personal power* in situations where Spanish is the major or dominant language spoken. If this motivates me enough to outweigh the inconvenience of going to class, I'll go ahead and devote the energy needed to learn it.

Creating interest like this is a great way to give yourself the motivation to attain your goals. How *you* create interest will depend on the variables of your own life, so each person will do it a little differently. The reasoning I used for learning Spanish is effective for me, and your own reasons will be effective for you.

Creating interest is a great way to give yourself the motivation to attain your goals.

Example — Learning Spanish

- Understand conversations overheard in my community

- Move freely and comfortably while traveling through Mexico

- Find the best prices while shopping in Mexican city plazas

- Ask directions easily in Spanish-speaking countries

- Develop an interest in other Romance languages

Let's look at a different type of example. Perhaps you'd like to go to graduate school, but you need to complete a few undergraduate courses in order to qualify for the program you want to enter. This can be a very difficult situation, not because the courses themselves are difficult but because they aren't always related to what you want to study.

Suppose you want to enter a graduate program in urban planning. Trouble is, you're required to take a lower-division course in statistics — a subject in which you have not the slightest interest. How can you *create* interest in it? By pinpointing what you will gain personally by taking this course.

Some possible benefits of knowing statistics are being able to spot and analyze trends in your business, and having a better understanding of news stories that report percentages. That's another way to improve your personal power. Or maybe you're a fan of a sport that's heavily statistical, like baseball or football. The statistics course might add a new dimension to your enjoyment of the game.

Creating interest has its intrinsic rewards too. When you create interest in a subject, you'll often find that it leads to new interests in other areas. Exploring these new areas leads to personal fulfillment as well as to other new interests — a chain reaction that goes on and on. A course in oceanography, for example, might lead you to an interest in saltwater aquariums, which leads to an interest in scuba diving, which leads to an interest in underwater photography — on and on until the underwater world is a source of never-ending exploration and fulfillment. Soon, your biggest challenge will be finding the time to pursue it all.

So on the surface, active learning may sound tiring, but it's actually *energizing*. Like jogging or swimming laps, sometimes you have to force yourself to do it, but once you get going you find yourself gathering more and more energy.

Now, before you read on, stop for a few moments and

When you create interest in a subject, you'll often find that it leads to new interests, creating a chain reaction that goes on and on.

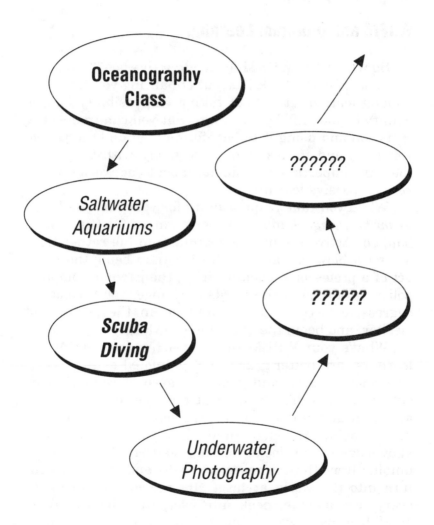

think about how you can create interest in the learning techniques you'll read about in this book. Go back to the contents page and look at each chapter title. How can you link the topic to what you do out in the real world? Specifically, how will it help *you* to have these skills?

(Remember, your answers will be purely personal and unlike those of any other reader, because your life is uniquely your own.)

WIIFM and Quantum Learning

So what's the WIIFM for reading this book?

Just this: The book is about enhancing your role as a lifelong learner. It's about taking responsibility for the quality of your life by learning what you can from every situation and using it to benefit yourself and the people you love, and to deal more effectively with the issues that are important to you. It's about "active learning" versus "passive learning."

When you take responsibility for your life, you begin to *make things happen* rather than just letting them happen. Active learning is leaning into life rather than letting it blow you around. Rather than being the product of a professor's teaching style, the pawn of company policy, or a reed in the winds of change, you become an aggressive force. You put yourself in the position of "seeker" and begin the quest for knowledge.

What's your WIIFM to be an active learner? Active learners earn better grades, get promoted more quickly, earn more money, and generally grab more enjoyment out of life. If you're in a quest for knowledge, you will automatically be open to the experiences and lessons life has to offer. An open mind absorbs and assimilates knowledge, then looks around eagerly for more. It unfolds from the introspective "self" and starts to venture into the world at large. Its passion is to explore every new avenue, peek into every tiny hidden alley, and follow every wandering road in search of knowledge.

When you take responsibility for your life, you begin to make things happen.

	Active Learning	vs.	Passive Learning

■ Learning what you can from every situation

       ■ Not seeing the learning potential

■ Using what you learn to your benefit

       ■ Ignoring the opportunities for growth from a learning experience

■ Making things happen

       ■ Letting things happen

■ Leaning into life

       ■ Pulling away from life

The more knowledge you have, the more choices you have when facing challenging situations. The more choices you have, the more personal power you have. And that's what this book is all about: *personal power*. It's the quiet kind of power you see in the eyes of people who are totally in charge of their own lives, in people who make decisions with confidence because they have the ability to gather all the information they need to make the *right* decisions for *themselves*.

This book will give you some proven, effective techniques for becoming an excellent learner. The WIIFM — the motivation — is purely personal for every individual who reads the book. Yet you must decide that the benefits outweigh the time and energy you'll spend — and time and energy *are* necessary to become a Quantum Learner! You must first make the commitment to open yourself to the techniques and exercises in the book, then practice them with the intention to make them a part of your life. Overall, no matter what your specific objective is, the WIIFM for reading this book has to be *"because it's worth it to me."*

Celebration

When you ask, "What's in it for me?" be sure to include *celebration* in your answer. Why?

Many times, as you look at a goal whose completion is still in the future, it seems larger than life — almost overwhelming. You think, "Wow, if I can accomplish that, what a great thing it will be." Later, when you finally do accomplish the goal, it doesn't seem so huge anymore. It becomes just another one of the things in your past, and you forget to acknowledge yourself for a job well done. You move on to the next project without stopping to reflect on the last one — without recognizing the significance of what you've just done.

When you've completed a task, it's important to celebrate the feat. It gives you a sense of accomplishment,

Having the ability to make decisions with confidence leads to personal power.

More knowledge

More Choices

Personal Power

completion, and confidence, and it builds motivation for your next goal. Celebration should be an essential aspect of your WIIFM.

Decide *before* you begin a project how you'll celebrate when you've finished it, and include small rewards as you complete individual steps along the way. For instance, you might decide to go out to dinner with a friend after reading and mastering the techniques in one chapter of this book, and treat yourself to a weekend away from home after completing the whole book.

In the SuperCamp corporate office, we do a lot of celebrating. Each time we reach an enrollment goal, we have a small party for office personnel, and an annual party to celebrate a successful summer of programs. We also try to include spontaneous get-togethers every so often.

My husband, Joe, and I had a marvelous celebration after we completed a challenging camp in Bear Valley, California. On our drive home we stopped at Yosemite National Park and opened a bottle of Dom Perignon. There we sat, in one of the most beautiful places on earth, sipping champagne and reflecting on the accomplishments of the summer, while waterfalls cascaded from the majestic mountains around us. The exhilaration of the moment was incredible, and as we drove the rest of the way home we felt energized for our next challenge.

Celebration should punctuate each significant step toward your goal and provide climactic excitement for a job well done.

"This Is It!"

How often has this happened to you: You're sitting in a staff meeting or lecture, gazing out the window, and a little voice in your head says something like, "This is *not* it. I'd rather be doing *anything* than sitting here right now."

Celebrate your completions!

It gives you a sense of:

■ Accomplishment

■ Completion

■ Confidence

■ Motivation for the next task

We all have a little voice like this, and we're masters at wanting to do something different or be somewhere other than where we are at the moment. We're masters at making things "*not* it."

When you were in elementary school, did you think, "This is not it, but junior high will be it." Then in junior high, did you think high school would be "it"? Lots of people remember going through this. When they finally got to high school, they found out that being a high school freshman *definitely* was not "it." Then they decided that being a senior would be "it." As seniors, they discovered that what would *really* be "it" would be going to college. Then in college, they thought being in the real world would be "it." When at long last they got to the real world, they wistfully recalled their college days and thought *that* was "it."

If you're like these people, pretty soon you've lived your whole life making things "not it." What does this kind of thinking cost you? Well, it costs you the quality of your life. Think of how much time you waste when you aren't focused on the task at hand — whether you're at a meeting and wishing you were at your own desk catching up, or on the golf course feeling guilty because you have piles of work on your desk. The voice in your head that keeps you from living totally in the *now* is the voice of your ego, the part of you that's always seeking comfort and convenience. But there's value in being *un*comfortable and *in*convenienced. For one thing, it moves your mind into a more active mode. And for another, it expands your comfort zone to include a wider array of experiences.

When you're at that "boring" meeting, think about how much more valuable you could make it if you really focused, became interested, and participated in the discussion. You could be surprised at the results. Similarly, when you're on the golf course or participating in some other leisure activity, imagine how much more you could enjoy it if you just relaxed, rather than thinking about all the work on your desk.

This is it! attitude influences a career.

Jake Gibbs was fresh out of Tennessee Technological University with a degree in electrical engineering when he was asked to join the country's largest computer services company. He eagerly accepted, thinking he'd immediately have a chance to use his newly acquired knowledge.

After several months on the job, however, Jake realized the work he was doing was closer to that of a draftsman than an engineer. Disillusioned and disappointed, he contemplated quitting so he could go on to something else — something that would really be "it." So he told his manager how he felt. He got this surprising reply.

"Look, I know you studied to be an engineer," the manager said, "and you think this is a waste of your time. But by doing the work of a draftsman now, you'll learn how to work with draftsmen and what to expect from them as the years go by. This will make you a more valuable engineer later."

Instead of looking elsewhere, Jake adopted the attitude that "this is it" and stayed on the job. Seventeen years later, as a manager for the same company, he attributes a large part of his career success to the fact that today he has the knowledge and ability to perform the job of almost every technical employee on his staff. Not only can he do these jobs, in many cases he already has, which makes it easier for him to relate to the challenges his staff faces.

The next time you're feeling, "This is not it," I invite you to try this: Tell yourself "This is *it!*" Say it *out loud,* with conviction! Practice on activities like washing the dishes, walking the dog, and cleaning up your desk. Live completely in the moment, and find value in whatever it is you're doing. Try for efficiency and perfection; pour everything you know into doing this job better than you ever did it before.

If you can learn how to make the most mundane situation or chore "it," you've learned how to put yourself into an ideal frame of mind for learning — receptive to details, feeling positive, and committed to being the best. The positive attitude you build with this simple little exercise will begin to infuse every area of your life, from simple, brief meetings to big, complex projects you didn't want to take on. And as an added benefit, you'll enjoy your leisure time more as well.

Now, as you go on to the rest of this book, say, "This is *it!* I'm going to get everything I can out of every chapter. I'm going to do every exercise as if it were the most important thing in the world. I'm going to give 100 percent to becoming a Quantum Learner. And when I finish reading the book and absorbing every ounce of benefit if offers, I'm going to *celebrate!*"

I Know I Know

☑ Check the box if you understand the concept:

☐ I know what "active learning" means, and why I want to be an active learner.

☐ I know how to "create interest" in my learning situations.

☐ I know how to make *anything* "it."

☐ I know the WIIFM for reading this book.

_____

_____

_____

_____

☐ After I read this book, I'm going to celebrate by:

_____

_____

_____

_____

4

Setting the Stage:

The Right Learning Environment

Why should you read this chapter?

✓ Establish an atmosphere that is comfortable and relaxing.

✓ Use music to be relaxed, alert, and ready to concentrate.

✓ Create and match moods with different types of music.

✓ Use visual reminders to maintain a positive attitude.

✓ Interact with your environment to become a better learner.

When you work in a properly arranged environment, it's much easier to develop and maintain a winning attitude. And a winning attitude makes for a much more successful learner.

When a stage crew is setting the stage for a play or musical production, it knows that attention to detail is important. The lighting, the sound, every nuance of color and shape determine the mood and help send the appropriate messages to the audience.

To the Quantum Learner, environmental factors are equivalent to the props a stage crew uses. The way you arrange your furniture, the music you use, your use of lighting, and the visual aids on your wall and bulletin board are all keys to creating the optimal learning environment.

If properly set up, your environment can be a valuable tool in building and maintaining a positive attitude. And as you'll learn in Chapter 5, a positive attitude is a valuable asset for learning.

By controlling your environment, you take an effective first step toward controlling your total learning experience. In fact, if I had to name the one reason why our programs are so successful in helping people become better learners, I would say it is because we strive to create an optimal environment both physically and emotionally.

Before a program begins, staff people go into each classroom and transform it into a place where students will be comfortable, stimulated, and supported. We bring in plants and music systems, and when necessary, we adjust the temperature and improve the lighting. We pad the chairs to make them more comfortable, wash the windows, and decorate the walls with beautiful posters and positive statements.

When the students enter this bright, comfortable, inviting physical environment on opening day, each one is greeted personally by his or her team leader. They're immediately drawn into playing games with others on

Create an optimal environment, both physically and emotionally.

Checklist:

❏ Furniture — type and arrangement

❏ Lighting

❏ Music

❏ Visuals — posters, pictures, bulletin board

❏ Placement of supplies

❏ Temperature

❏ Plants

❏ Comfort

❏ General mood

the team, so they start right off with a sense of belonging. Their all-important first experiences are pleasant and happy.

Gradually, over the next couple of days, through the use of communication exercises and other group activities, they get to know the others on their team very well. We make them feel comfortable with themselves as individuals and as group members. In this safe environment, they open themselves to stretching their comfort zones and trying new things — and that's an ideal state of mind for optimal learning. Only after taking special care to produce this state of mind do we introduce them to the academic skills that help them do better in school.

You can set up an ideal environment for yourself just as easily, both in your own home and in your place of business. Here's how to do it.

The Microenvironment: Your Work and Creativity Space

It all starts with the personal area you occupy when you work, study, and learn. Turning this space into an optimal environment is something only you can do, because only you can arrange the details in a way that feels right for you.

In Chapter 6 you'll learn about your personal style of receiving, perceiving, and processing information — that is, your learning style. Another aspect of your learning style is how lighting, music, and room design affect you. The goal is to create an atmosphere that induces comfort and relaxation, because it's in a state of "relaxed focus" that you concentrate best and are able to learn most easily. Tense muscles divert your blood supply — *and* your attention.

Your home is probably a good place to start, since there you have the most freedom to change and experiment. You probably have a more intimate sense of "belonging" in your home as well, and it's good to begin

An ideal state of mind for optimal learning is created when you are willing to stretch your comfort zone and try new things.

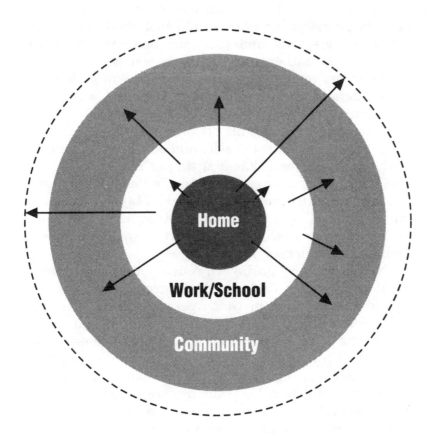

Start from a safe and secure home environment.

building your safety zone outward from a place like this. After you succeed at building the perfect learning environment in your home, you can take the things that work for you there and apply them at your office or other work space away from home.

It's best to claim a separate space for yourself somewhere in your home. That way you'll be better able to head off distractions. If you don't have a studio or den, find a quiet corner you can section off, a section of the garage that doesn't get much traffic, an attic room, an extra-large closet, or even an old tool shed behind the house. Be creative, and use your imagination to see what *could* be rather than what's there now.

After you've claimed your space, you can go to work on the details. Some people prefer a formal work environment, while others are more comfortable in an unstructured area. Think of situations in which you were able to concentrate easily and do a great amount of work without stress. Was it sitting at a desk facing the wall? Sprawling over cushions on the floor? Sitting at a kitchen table in front of a window? Maybe you like a combination of structured and unstructured, like doing your reading and research while sitting in an easy chair, then moving to a desk for writing.

Next, consider lighting. Of course, your space should be lit well enough that you don't strain your eyes, but this is another area in which personal preference controls. Some like a room that is uniformly bright, while others like a light focused on what they're doing at the moment. Still others like a combination of lighting effects. Because lighting can be an expensive project, you might want to notice your preference when you are in various offices, classrooms, and the homes of friends before investing in something yourself.

Here are some other important details to consider in your physical environment.

Think of situations in which you were able to concentrate easily.

For some it takes a very formal, structured environment:

■ Desk

■ Desk chair

■ Specific place

■ Orderly work area

Others like an unstructured area:

■ Kitchen table

■ Easy chair

■ Use of several areas

■ Everything out where they can see it

- a bulletin board where you can put visual aids to prompt your thought process — like charts of work now in progress and lists of possible projects
- a shelf for books and reference materials
- a "capture system" for recording thoughts that occur to you and might be useful later, like a notebook or a tape recorder
- a daily planner to organize your time
- a stereo or other music system
- positive affirmations to keep you in the "winning attitude" frame of mind

The last two items are so important to an optimal learning environment, they deserve separate attention.

Music — The Key to Quantum Learning

The reason music is so important to the Quantum Learning environment is that it actually corresponds to and affects your physiological conditions. During heavy mental work, your pulse and blood pressure tend to rise. Your brain waves speed up, and your muscles become tense. During relaxation and meditation, your pulse and blood pressure decrease, and your muscles relax. Normally, it's difficult to concentrate when you're deeply relaxed, and it's difficult to relax when you're concentrating intently.

Dr. Georgi Lozanov, whose accelerated learning techniques are the basis for SuperCamp, sought a way to combine strenuous mental work with relaxed physiology in order to produce excellent learners. After intensive experimentation with students, he found that music was the key. *Relaxation induced by specific music leaves the mind alert and able to concentrate.*

The music Dr. Lozanov found most conducive to this state is baroque music, like that of Bach, Handel, Pachelbel, and Vivaldi. These composers used very specific beats and patterns that automatically synchronize

Using specific music allows you to do strenuous mental work while remaining relaxed and focused.

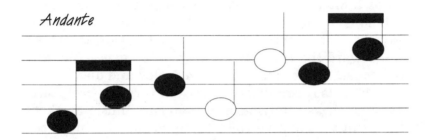

Strenuous Mental Work

Without music	With appropriate music
▩ Pulse and blood pressure rise	▩ Pulse and blood pressure decrease
▩ Brain waves speed up	▩ Brain waves slow down
▩ Muscles tense	▩ Muscles relax

our minds with our bodies. For instance, most baroque music is timed at sixty beats per minute, which is the same as an average resting heart rate. Many contemporary musicians are amazed at how their peers of three hundred years ago were able to compose pieces with such mathematical precision.

As you might know, the influence of baroque music is not limited to humans; in experiments, plants grew lush foliage and large roots when baroque music was played to them, and they even leaned toward the music as if toward the sun. (By the way, when exposed to acid rock music, these same plants shriveled and died.)

It has also been theorized that in very left-brain situations such as studying new material, music awakens the intuitive, creative right brain so that its input can be integrated into the whole process. It is your right brain that tends to be distracted during meetings, lectures, and the like, which is why you'll sometimes find yourself daydreaming and gazing at the view when you meant to pay attention. Playing music is an effective way to occupy your right brain while concentrating on left-brain activities.

At SuperCamp, we use an effective blend of music for different activities and purposes. We use it to *set* a mood as well as to *match* it. For instance, when students are concentrating on an academic subject, there is most often baroque music played at low volume in the background. During breaks (which are frequent) we play loud, upbeat popular music because it encourages physical activity like dancing, tossing a Frisbee around, or playing hackysack. It also helps to create a positive, upbeat mood. A few minutes of this helps the students focus more intently when class resumes. I encourage you to try using baroque music while you're working, studying, and creating. If you can, include a stereo system or a small audiocassette player in your work environment.

Positive statements hung on your walls are constant reminders of your potential and greatness.

" *Whatever you can do,*
or dream you can do,
begin it.
Boldness has genius,
power, and magic in it. "

— *Goethe*

Following Positive Signs

When I say positive signs, I'm talking about visual stimuli reminding you that you're capable of excelling. Here are some items you can use in your work area.

"Thought Starters," Like Quotes and Snappy Slogans

The following quote by Goethe has hung on the wall of our office for many years: "Whatever you can do, or dream you can do, begin it. Boldness has genius, power, and magic in it."

You can find thought starters in books of quotes, newspapers, and many other places. In Chapter 5, I list a number of them that you can make into signs and hang strategically in your space.

Certificates and Awards You Have Earned

Diplomas, "best sales rep" awards, trophies for athletic achievement, and all kinds of other awards are great reminders that you're a talented and capable soul.

"Peak Moment" Props

A peak moment is a time in your life when you did something exceptionally well; it includes the jubilation that accompanied it. We often see peak moment photos in the sports section of the newspaper; it's the moment of triumph that photographers love to capture. If you happen to have a photo of yourself at a peak moment, this is a perfect affirmation for your work area. Otherwise, you can recreate the feeling with a written description, or by framing a memento from the occasion. Many writers frame the cover of each of their published books. Small business owners frequently frame and hang the first dollar they ever made from the business.

It is especially powerful to hang photos or momentoes of your peak moments, as well as awards and notes of appreciation.

- Trophies

- Plaques

- Certificates

- Acknowledgments

- Photos of:
  - Completions
  - Competitions
  - Challenges

Notes, Gifts, and Cards of Appreciation from Friends and Colleagues

In this busy world, if someone takes the time to let you know how much they appreciate you, you know they mean it. Keeping their words and gifts visible helps you acknowledge yourself once in a while too.

I know a writer who keeps in her appointment calendar a special card she received from an older sister who couldn't make it to her first book-signing party. The card reads, "To someone who's never seen a mountain too high to climb." It's signed, "With love — and admiration." To this writer, the card represents a memory of a peak moment and all the joy and celebration that surrounded it.

Be on the lookout for positive affirmations. Everybody needs a few of them in their personal work space to maintain a positive attitude when the going gets tough. They make you feel valued and supported, which is important to your self-esteem.

The Macroenvironment — Out in the Big World

So far, we've been talking about the microenvironment, or that small area that is completely yours and under your exclusive control. If you can make your personal work space an area in which you feel completely safe, comfortable, and valued, it will act as a powerful anchor when you move from there out into the world. Little by little, you'll be able to stretch your safety zone and thus expand your sphere of influence and personal power into the macroenvironment. You have less control over what happens in the macroenvironment, yet you *do* decide the degree to which you will interact with the world at large.

Dr. Marian Diamond, in her research with laboratory rats, found that those that lived in an enriched environment were better learners. (By "enriched envi-

Your level of participation in the world at large can determine your ability to learn with ease.

An enriched environment

produces better learners in problem-solving situations.

An impoverished environment

produces slow, uninterested learners.

ronment," she meant one in which the rats had positive attention from their keepers and access to toys that stimulated their thinking.) At all ages, from birth until old age, these so-called enriched rats were better learners in many problem-solving situations than rats who lived in impoverished environments.

If Dr. Diamond had studied human beings, she would have found similar phenomena. Her reason for conducting these experiments on rats, however, lies in the fact that she wished to study the effect of the environment on the anatomy and physiology of the brain. What she found was that by controlling the environment, she was actually able to produce structural changes in the brain! Specifically, with environmental stimulation, the brain cells in the neocortex (the seat of higher cognitive functioning) actually became larger. Just by introducing environmental changes, she was able to effect this change, which she correlates to better performance — even in rats that had already lived a good portion of their lives under unfavorable conditions. The best results were seen when toys were changed about twice a week, so that mastery of one thing led not to boredom but to new challenges.

Two other scientists did experiments in which some rats were able to watch the enriched rats playing with toys in another cage. They found that *passive observation is not enough*. The observers showed no improvement in learning ability and were less curious than those who could play with the toys themselves. In order to become better learners and problem-solvers, they had to interact with the environment themselves.

What does this all mean for you? It has been found that there are a lot of similarities in the brain physiology and body chemistry of rats and humans. (That's one reason rats are used so extensively for all kinds of research.) The experiments just described suggest that the more you interact with the environment, the more proficient you'll become in dealing with challenging situ-

The more you interact with the environment, the more proficient you'll become at dealing with challenging situations and the more easily you'll be able to learn new information.

Abundant opportunities exist to interact with the world.

Take a risk! Go for it!

ations and the more easily you'll be able to learn new information. Why? Because each time you relate actively with new stimuli in your environment, you build on your personal storehouse of knowledge, which gives you just that much more information to use in approaching the next situation.

You have abundant opportunities to interact with the environment and an immense variety of input to absorb from the world. It's possible to learn something from every kind of interaction, from digging in a garden to taking a night class to learning how to climb mountains. So go out and be active. Take the risk and do something new!

To take a simple example, let's say you decide to turn the little chunk of earth you call your backyard into a place of botanical beauty, where you can sit on a summer morning with the newspaper or proudly invite friends for a barbecue and tall cool drinks. What kind of interaction would this involve? Well, it might start with looking through magazines for ideas, and checking out some gardening books from the library. Next, you might take a list of plants and other materials to your local nursery or landscaping store and talk to someone who knows a great deal about the subject. After learning as much as you can, you make the commitment to purchase the materials and take them home. There, as you work with the earth, molding the yard into the wonderful place you envisioned, you learn about the physical environment — what creatures live in the earth, for instance, and how much effort it takes to dig a hole. As you maintain your little Eden, you keep learning more and more and more. Basic as it may seem, this is all information that can potentially be used in other situations.

Interacting with the environment also means taking opportunities when they come — and *making* opportunities when they don't come. If friends invite you to go out on their boat and learn how to water ski, give it some

Taking advantage of opportunities as they arise, or creating them, will expand your safety zone and your personal knowledge.

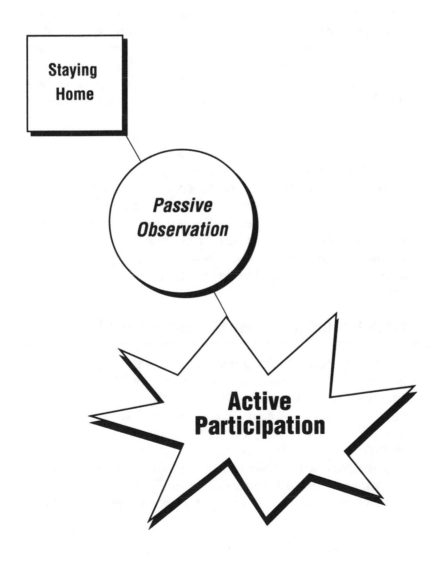

Staying Home

Passive Observation

Active Participation

serious consideration. Remember, active participation is better than passive observation. (Of course, even going out to watch is better than staying home.) If you have watched folks floating by in their hot-air balloons and always thought, "Ah, someday I'd like to try that," make it happen! If you've always wanted to learn more about something and you find out there's a seminar on it, make arrangements to attend.

Finally, interacting with the environment means embracing change. It's nice and safe and easy to maintain the status quo. It takes lots of stretching to step beyond it to something new. The stretch you make from changing something in your life, like taking a new job, will expand your safety zone and your personal knowledge bank. It will also open your eyes to new things in the environment.

Dr. Diamond's finding that rats can become better learners even at advanced ages with enriched environments has implications for you too. It means that no matter what your age, from child to senior citizen, there's something you can do *right now* to become a better learner. So if there's something you've always dreamed of doing, go out and do it! You'll have the satisfaction of having accomplished something, and you'll make a step toward Quantum Learning at the same time.

Consolidation (or "Time to Take a Break")

At SuperCamp, frequent breaks are a requirement for every kind of learning session. Breaks are so important that we sometimes even let the students decide when it's break time; if one person raises a hand and asks for a break, that's a sign everyone could benefit from it.

There are a number of reasons for this; I'll mention several. One, *in any learning session, you remember best the information you learn first and last.* So it follows

A supportive environment contributes to recovery.

A powerful downhill skier and member of the U.S. Development Ski Team, Muffy Davis had always based her self-image on her ability on the slopes. In February 1989, during a practice run on the Mount Baldy training course in Sun Valley, Idaho, that image was shattered. Muffy careened off the trail, flew through the air at fifty-five miles per hour, and crashed into a nearby tree. The accident left her paralyzed from the waist down.

During her three and a half months of recovery and rehabilitation, Muffy's hospital room became a supportive environment that funneled all her energy into healing. Surrounded by supportive props of all kinds — pictures of family and friends, flowers, stuffed animals, and computer-printed banners from friends and classmates that read WE LOVE YOU, MUFFY, and HERE'S TO A SPEEDY RECOVERY — she began to mend.

She also converted that hospital room into a campaign headquarters, running a successful video campaign for junior class president, then serving in absentia. Following her hospital stay, she returned to school a senior, was elected student body president, and graduated from high school with a 3.93 GPA.

Though still in a wheelchair, Muffy's now back to playing sports. Special equipment lets her play tennis and water ski, and she's learning to downhill ski again.

Currently a student at Stanford, Muffy plans to study medicine and specialize in the mind-body connection that helped her to recover from her accident. She's still dedicated to creating a positive environment for herself as a powerful support system. Though her doctors won't make any guarantees, Muffy is confident she'll walk again. And, knowing her, of course she will.

that if you take many breaks, you'll remember more of the total information. Many short breaks mean more "firsts" and "lasts." Two, when your mind becomes fatigued, the change of mental state that a break ensures will revitalize your brain cells for the next stretch.

A break is also *time to consolidate,* to assimilate new information and let it settle solidly into your conscious and subconscious minds. If you're actively working and interacting in the big world, or macroenvironment, taking a break means stepping back into the comfort zone of your personal space, or microenvironment. In this stress-free place you can rest, relax, and internalize whatever you've been doing out in the world.

If you're working at home or in your office, taking a break usually means getting up from your desk or chair and doing something else for a short time. Change your music to something fast and upbeat, then dance or do some aerobics for ten minutes. Or go for a walk, run up and down the stairs a few times, lie on the grass and watch the clouds, play with your dog — anything to change your physical and mental pace for a while.

Quantum Learning is a well-balanced interplay between work and play, between internal and external stimulation, and between time spent inside your safety zone and stepping out of it. Whether you're at home, in your office, at the library, or somewhere else out there in the world, be aware of the control you have over environmental details and how you choose to interact with them. Because how you control your environment goes a long way toward determining how you will learn.

I Know I Know

✓ Check the box if you understand the concept:

☐ I know a place in my home where I can make a space for work and creativity.

☐ I know what kind of furniture and lighting I need to do my best thinking.

☐ I know that music can help me concentrate during a learning session.

☐ I know four positive signs I can use in my work space to fuel my mind.

1 _____

2 _____

3 _____

4 _____

☐ I know I'll be a better learner if I interact constructively with my environment.

☐ I know that I need breaks from activity to get the most from learning sessions, both in my personal space and out in the big world.

5

Cultivating a
Winning Attitude:

What Would You Do
If You Knew
You Couldn't Fail?

Why should you read this chapter?

 Understand how F stands for *feedback* rather than *failure*.

 Choose your reactions and self-talk to create high motivation.

 Overcome barriers by providing yourself with positive messages.

 Control your frame of mind by controlling bodily and facial expressions.

Thinking like a winner makes you a winner. That's why it's so important to know how to cultivate a winning attitude. In this chapter you'll learn how to turn negatives into positives and limitations into opportunities.

When it comes to learning, what's your most valuable asset? Is it your intelligence? Your genes? How about your education?

These all have a role in your ability to learn, yet there is something else that can affect the learning process more than all of them put together. Your most valuable asset is a *positive attitude.*

If you have high expectations for yourself, high self-esteem, and the belief that you will succeed, you will have high achievement. It's an old saying, and it's still true: What you think about, comes about. As Henry Ford put it, "Whether you think you can, or think you can't — you're right." Think like a winner, and you will win.

Decide to have a positive attitude, and things begin to change immediately. Possibilities become probabilities, and limitations become opportunities. As you remember from our discussion about the brain in Chapter 2, positive emotions smooth the way toward success.

What are some of the things you would try if you *knew* you couldn't fail? Start your own business? Make a career change? Write a book? Go back to school? I'd like you to stop reading now and think of four things you'd like to accomplish in your life. *Please stop here.*

Decide to have a positive attitude, and things begin to change immediately.

What would you do if you knew you couldn't fail?

1. _____

2. _____

3. _____

4. _____

Now, what are some of the things that hold you back from doing these things? Many times, the culprit is fear: fear of failure, fear of rejection, fear of stepping out of your comfort zone into risky new territory. Fear is like an invisible barrier that can keep you forever fenced in to a life without challenge, adventure, exhilaration, wonder, or celebration. In short, it will keep you from exploring and discovering your limitless ability.

When it comes to doing the things on your list, you're not only a very powerful person, you're the *only* person who can make these things happen for you.

Inside of you, from the time you were an infant, has been a person who is naturally curious, who wants to go 100 percent for satisfaction in life, who wants to take the risks involved to live a life filled with accomplishment, joy, energy, and radiance.

As a tiny child who moved around by crawling, you watched older people walking and decided to try it. Little by little, you developed the skills you needed to learn to walk. First you learned to pull yourself to a standing position, then you learned how to balance on your two little feet; then you moved a few steps as you held on to a table or your parents' fingers. As you learned each of these skills, you fumbled many times, sometimes painfully. Yet did you ever stop and think, "Well, I guess I'm just not a walker. I'll just crawl for the rest of my life"? Of course not! You kept trying, learning from each day's trials and making little changes in your technique until one day you were able to take a few steps on your own. From those few steps, you were soon toddling all over the place, with the notion in your happy little brain that walking was just as natural as could be.

Failure = Feedback

What's important about that learning experience in walking is the way you viewed failure. It wasn't a big, horrible, negative thing that made you feel bad or stu-

Inside of you is the person who wants to live life to its fullest.

Accomplishment

Joy

Energy

Radiance

pid and blocked you from the pursuit of your goal. When you fell down, you didn't think, "Oh, I'm so embarrassed! I hope Mommy didn't see me!" Instead, each little failure was another piece of information leading you to success. It was the feedback you needed to make necessary changes in your technique. Only when you had learned everything you could from each failure could you correct your mistakes and move on to your ultimate success.

You can go about accomplishing your goals now the same way you accomplished the goal of learning how to walk. In fact, if it weren't for the multitude of negative messages that assail you every day, you would probably go through life knowing that you could do whatever you decided to do, regardless of the difficulty rating.

While you were learning to walk, you probably had lots of encouragement from the adults in your life — or if not outright encouragement, at least there wasn't anyone there telling you, "Forget it — you'll never be able to learn it anyhow." Later on in your life, however, the negative comments and feedback started to roll in. Most of the time it was probably unintentional on the part of the person doling it out. Often, it was just someone with the best intentions, trying to ease your pain.

Maybe you came home from school one day upset because you couldn't get a basketball through the hoop, and your mother said, "Don't worry, sweetheart. Not everybody is good at basketball." It's an innocent comment, yet hidden in it is the implication that you shouldn't waste your time because you'll never be good at it.

Simple things like this are the beginning of negative attitudes. By the time you're a teenager, you're pretty clear that there are a lot of things you're *not*. If you have taken to heart all the things well-meaning people have told you, you've concluded that you're not a tennis player, because you tried a few times to hit the ball over the net, failed, and gave up. You're not a math whiz,

Only when you have learned everything possible from each failure can you move on to your ultimate success.

Failure = Feedback

A
N
D

L
E
A
D
S

T
O

Success

you're not a public speaker, you're not a singer, you're not an artist . . . in fact, you aren't sure what you are, because you don't have the confidence to try anything long enough to become successful at it. You let failure become a negative cycle that pulls you down and drains you of energy.

Along the road to proficiency in any subject or skill, from playing basketball to programming a computer to flying an airplane, there are times when you fumble because you've not yet mastered an important aspect of it. If you take a fumble as a sign that says, "I can't do this," then you'll be absolutely right — you can't do it. If, on the other hand, you take a fumble merely as feedback — as information — it takes on a whole new meaning. All you have to do is learn from this information, then make the appropriate changes in your technique. That way you'll eventually succeed. It's that simple.

The only failure in life is the failure to try. Now, think of each of the four things you wrote down earlier in the chapter. Is any of them such a worthless endeavor that you can resolve not even to try it?

Self-Talk – The Psychology of a Positive Attitude

Remember Jack Canfield's study, in which he found that every day we receive six times as many negative as positive messages? What would your life be like if those figures were reversed?

Of course, the world is not suddenly going to start throwing bucketfuls of compliments your way for no reason. In the beginning, *you* have to be the one to give yourself pats on the back. Along the road to a successful, fulfilled life, you must give yourself the go-ahead, the positive feedback, and the rewards for success. In short, you have to take responsibility for your own life experience.

Imagine you've just walked into a party. You've arrived early and it's still kind of slow, like most parties

What things have you decided you're not good at, after giving them only a try or two?

Mastery takes practice and repetition.

The only failure in life is the failure to participate.

are in the beginning. And like most parties, this one has the potential to become either really exciting or excruciatingly boring. You decide which it's going to be. You can say, "This is going to be a drag," and then hang out anyhow, letting yourself be bored to a dull haze. Or you can say, "Hey, this is going to be the best party I'll be at all day, and I'm going to make sure it's worthwhile!" Then, decide what's needed to make it live up to your expectations — and *go for it!*

In *any* situation, we can imagine any number of possible scenarios. Has this ever happened to you? You pass one of your coworkers in the hallway at work, smile, and say hello, and the person walks right by without acknowledging you. You could make up hundreds of possible scenarios to explain this if you had the time and the inclination. Here are two possibilities: "He must be angry at me for some reason, to ignore me like that," and "She must be very preoccupied about that project she's working on to walk right by without hearing or seeing me."

One of these interpretations is going to produce negative, self-defeating thoughts in your mind, while the other will produce neutral or positive thoughts. When you choose negative energy, it affects how you view yourself, as well as the quality of your relationship with that person. But if you always choose the most positive scenario, your frame of mind will be conducive to success and effective relationships.

This applies to expectations as well as to explanations. When you expect the best, you're inviting the best to become reality. Expect the worst, and you're inviting disaster.

Even when there are variables over which you have no control, such as the weather, inflation, interest rates, and the like, there's still room for you to move around mentally. Since you have a choice, why not make up the most positive outcome you can think of? Only when you have a picture in mind of how good things could be, can

In any situation, you can imagine any number of possible scenarios.

negative,
self-defeating
thought

positive,
uplifting
thought

Why not pick the better one?

you begin to make it reality.

Although you aren't always in control of the circumstances, you're totally and absolutely in control of how you react to them. If you have a tendency to walk into situations and think, "Oh, man, this is going to be boring," I ask you to make a simple change in the way you talk to yourself. Instead of saying "I'm bored," say "I am choosing to be bored." You *do* choose your reactions, and the way you talk to yourself can make you high or make you low.

Knowing this can cause an immediate shift in your attitude, and once you see how easy it is to affect your own state of mind with the words you use to talk to yourself, imagine the difference it will make when you begin to talk yourself *up* rather than talk yourself *down*.

If you don't believe you're a powerful person or that words can make a world of difference, try this experiment. Think of someone you know who could use an attitude boost. Now, for each of five days, think of something positive you can say to that person, then do it. For instance, if a fellow worker or student seems really timid, think of five things that you really like about her. Point out one of them to her each day. If your seven-year-old lacks self-confidence at school, find five things he's done well and compliment him on it. Maybe your spouse has been a little down lately; say something especially supportive and positive each day before work.

After five days, notice the difference in that person's attitude when the two of you come into contact. If *one* person (you) is powerful enough to make a difference with *one* little comment a day, think how much your own attitude can change if you constantly give yourself positive suggestions and feedback. Here are some positive messages you can give yourself to overcome barriers along the way to your goals.

- I know I can make this work.
- My mind is uniquely capable.

Expect the best, and you invite the best to become reality.

Picture in your mind how good things can be.

- I'm committed to mastering this.
- Everything is supporting me in reaching my goal.
- The more I practice, the better I get.
- I learn something from every mistake.
- Now I'm really going for it.
- I get better every day.
- Now I'm on the right track.
- This is fun!
- My brain is in high gear.
- I'm really proud of myself.

At the end of Chapters 3 through 11 in this book, I've included a list titled "I Know I Know." Each list enables you to review the chapter and point out to yourself just how much you've learned by reading it. The I Know I Know's are equivalent to positive self-talk, so be sure to go through them. They're a great way to keep your attitude humming along in high gear and to validate to yourself that you know the information.

How Physiology Can Help

I once watched a little girl playing a board game in which the players were challenged to do various things in order to gain points. She spun the arrow and moved her piece on the board to a square that read, "Pretend to cry for five points. Give yourself twenty-five points if you can produce real tears." From a perfectly cheerful, bouncing demeanor, the girl began to slump. Her face fell, her chin trembled, and tears fell down her face, all in less than twenty seconds. I was amazed at how quickly she could change and the effect it had on her.

Some months later, I was feeling depressed about a challenging situation. It was a gloomy day, but I decided to take my lunch outside and eat in a small park near my office. As I sat there eating a sandwich and feeling sorry for myself, a group of young people pranced by,

Breakthroughs happen in both physical and mental challenges.

Craig Francisco knew he was no Arnold Palmer. In fact, he needed to work on so many aspects of his golf game that he was almost overwhelmed by the challenge. He was surprised he even made the golf team.

"I thought I'd never be a very good player," he said, "so I didn't even practice." But a mental breakthrough taught him just how much power his mind could have over his total experience — and the result was a greatly improved golf game.

His breakthrough occurred during a training program in which he learned how to use his bare hands to break through one-inch-thick pine boards. Before beginning, he was asked to write on the front of his board a barrier he felt he wanted to "break through" so he could achieve more in life.

Craig knew he was subconsciously keeping himself from doing many things by telling himself he couldn't do them, so on his board he wrote "subconscious mind." Like many others, when he broke through the board, he felt the exhilaration of major accomplishment.

"As soon as I did it, I knew I could do anything I wanted to do. Nothing could get in my way," he said.

He returned home and worked on his golf game for the rest of the summer. His efforts helped take his team to first place in the league, the region, and the district during the following year. In fact, they went on to place sixth in the entire state of Ohio. Craig Francisco, who formerly considered himself a poor golfer, was first man on the team and was voted most valuable player. He personally won eleven trophies over the season, and he helped his team win nine more.

"I really learned to believe in myself, and that anything's possible if I put my mind to it." For Craig, a positive attitude made all the difference.

bouncing and laughing and generally emitting a sense of joy in life that everybody in the park seemed to notice. I got up and walked around for twenty minutes or so, trying to put as much energy and bounce into my walk as I could. By the time I got back to the office, I felt positively revitalized and ready to take some immediate, positive steps to remedy my situation.

Your body usually takes cues from your mind, but you can also use your body to *give* cues to your mind. By this I mean that you can control your frame of mind by controlling your body. Here's an exercise you can do to prove this is true.

Right now, slump way down in your chair. Tilt your head down, cross your arms and pull into yourself. Stick out your lips in a pout, let your cheeks droop, and tense the muscles around your eyes. Now try to feel happy and optimistic. Can you do it? I doubt it.

Now turn the situation around. This time, sit up straight in your chair. Throw back your head and shoulders. Let a smile play around the corners of your mouth, and widen your eyes. Cock your head a little bit. Now try to feel sad. Can you do it? I doubt it. (If you do start to succeed, check your posture — I'll bet it's starting to slump again.)

You can use this exercise for a positive, self-confident attitude during study sessions, in meetings, when you give presentations, and in social situations. Often, the way you participate is a direct result of the way you feel. And the way you feel is a result of the way you hold yourself. Many times we have to make a conscious effort to notice our posture and to change from that self-defeating slump to sitting tall.

And Now, On to Becoming an Excellent Learner

As you read the rest of the book, check in with yourself often to make sure your attitude is in high gear. Always think of the best possible scenario when you pic-

Controlling your frame of mind is possible by controlling your body.

Follow this exercise to prove it:

First:

- Slump way down in your chair.

- Tilt your head down, cross your arms, and pull into yourself.

- Stick out your lips in a pout, let your cheeks drop, and tense the muscles around your eyes.

- Try to feel happy and optimistic.

Second:

- Sit up straight in your chair.

- Throw back your head and shoulders.

- Let a smile play around the corners of your mouth and widen your eyes.

- Now try to feel sad and depressed.

ture yourself as a Quantum Learner. Remember to regard your fumbles as feedback along your road to success, and give yourself pats on the back when you master something.

I Know I Know

☑ Check the box if you understand the concept:

☐ I know that my most valuable asset for learning success is:

_____

☐ I know that failure is simply the information I need to succeed.

☐ I know five messages I can use to talk myself up:

1 _____

2 _____

3 _____

4 _____

5 _____

☐ I know how to use my body to attain a positive attitude.

☐ I know I am a powerful person.

6

Discovering Your
Personal Learning Style

Why should you read this chapter?

 Discover the ways people learn.

 Learn how *you* perceive and process
information.

 Utilize techniques to balance your learning
style and achieve learning success.

 Detect learning styles of others in your life.

Your personal learning style is a key to improved performance on the job, in school, and in interpersonal situations. When you're aware of how you and others perceive and process information, you can make learning and communication easier by working *with* your own style.

In some primary and secondary schools in the United States, teachers are realizing that every person has an optimum way of learning new information. They understand that some students need to be taught in ways that vary from standard teaching methods. If these pupils are taught in the standard way, they are less likely to comprehend what's being presented. Knowing these different learning styles has helped teachers everywhere reach all or nearly all of their students simply by presenting information in several different ways.

Rita Dunn, a pioneer in the field of learning styles, has identified many variables that affect how people learn. These include physical, emotional, sociological, and environmental factors. Some people learn best, for example, when the light is bright, while others learn better in low light. Some learn best when working with peers, while others prefer an authority figure such as a parent or teacher; still others find that working alone is the most effective for them. Some need background sound, such as music, while others cannot concentrate unless the room is silent. Some need a structured, neatly organized work environment, while others like to spread everything out where they can see it.

Working independently, various learning style researchers in fields ranging from psychology to management training have made discoveries that reinforce one another with amazing consistency.

Though different researchers have devised different terminology and have found various ways to break down individual learning styles, it is generally agreed there are two major categories of how we learn. First, how we *perceive* information most easily (modality), and second,

Your learning style is a combination of how you perceive, then organize and process information.

Modality

How you perceive information the most easily

Brain Dominance

How you organize and process information

how we *organize and process* that information (brain dominance). A person's learning style is a combination of how he or she perceives, then organizes and processes information.

When you're familiar with your personal learning style, you can take important steps to help yourself learn faster and more easily. Plus, learning how to decipher the learning styles of others, like your boss, colleagues, teacher, spouse, parents, and children, can help you strengthen your rapport with them.

At the beginning of a learning experience, one of our first steps is to identify a person's modality as visual, auditory, or kinesthetic (V-A-K). As these terms suggest, visual people learn through what they see, auditory learners from what they hear, and kinesthetic learners from movement and touching. Although each of us learns in all three of these modalities to some degree, *most* people prefer one over the other two.

Michael Grinder, author of *Righting the Education Conveyor Belt*, has taught learning and teaching styles to many instructors. He notes that in every group of thirty students, an average of twenty-two are able to learn effectively enough visually, auditorily, *and* kinesthetically that they don't need any special attention. Of the remaining eight students, about six prefer one of the modalities over the other two so strongly that they struggle to understand the instructions most of the time, unless special care is taken to present it in their preferred mode. For these people, knowing their best learning modality can mean the difference between success and failure. The remaining two students have difficulty learning due to external causes.

Visual, Auditory, or Kinesthetic?

Do you often catch yourself saying things like "That looks right to me," or "I get the picture"? Or are you more likely to say "That sounds right to me," or "That

Learning modalities:

 Visual

Learning through seeing

 Auditory

Learning through hearing

 **Kinesthetic**

Learning through moving, doing, and touching

rings a bell"? Expressions like these may be clues to your preferred modality.

If you couldn't see or hear, or if you couldn't feel texture, shape, temperature, weight, or resistance in the environment, you would literally have no way of learning. Most of us learn in many ways, yet we usually favor one modality over the others. Many people don't realize they are favoring one way, because nothing external tells them they're any different from anyone else. Knowing that there *are* differences goes a long way toward explaining things like why we have problems understanding and communicating with some people and not with others, and why we handle some situations more easily than others.

How do you discover your own preferred modality? One simple way is to listen for clues in your speech, as in the expressions above. Another way is to notice your behavior when you attend a seminar or workshop. Do you seem to get more from reading the handout or from listening to the presenter? Auditory people prefer listening to the material and sometimes get lost if they try to take notes on the subject during the presentation. Visual people prefer to read the handouts and look at the illustrations the presenter puts on the board. They also take excellent notes. Kinesthetic learners do best with "hands on" activities and group interaction.

Suppose you've just purchased a new barbecue grill. It comes in thirty-five separate pieces, accompanied by a twelve-page instruction booklet to help you assemble it. How do you manage this? Does everything you read in the booklet seem vague and unclear until you look at the illustration and start putting the pieces together yourself? Or does the opposite happen: You're baffled by the array of parts, but when you read the instructions, everything seems perfectly clear?

If you need to start working with the parts physically, you're probably a kinesthetic learner. If reading the instructions clarifies things for you, you're most

When assembling something, which method do you prefer?

Visual

Follow the illustrations?
Read the directions?

Auditory

Have someone talk you through it?

Kinesthetic

Start putting it together yourself?

likely visual. If you can't make it work from instructions or drawings, but when you call the company and someone tells you how to put the thing together, it all begins to make sense, that's a definite clue that your style is auditory.

Many other behavioral traits are clues to your preference as well. The following characteristics will help you zero in on your best learning modality.

Visual People

- are neat and orderly
- speak quickly
- are good long-range planners and organizers
- are observant of environmental detail
- are appearance-oriented in both dress and presentation
- are good spellers and can actually see the words in their minds
- remember what was seen, rather than heard
- memorize by visual association
- usually are not distracted by noise
- have trouble remembering verbal instructions unless they are written down and often ask people to repeat themselves
- are strong, fast readers
- would rather read than be read to
- need an overall view and purpose and are cautious until mentally clear about an issue or project
- doodle during phone conversations and staff meetings
- forget to relay verbal messages to others
- often answer questions with a simple yes or no
- would rather do a demonstration than make a speech
- like art more than music
- often know what to say but can't think of the right words
- sometimes tune out when they mean to pay attention

Knowing the characteristics of visual, auditory, and kinesthetic learners will help you zero in on *your* best learning modality.

Visual

- Do you doodle when you talk on the phone?
- Do you speak quickly?
- Would you rather see a map than hear directions?

Auditory

- Do you talk to yourself?
- Do you prefer a lecture or seminar to reading a book?
- Do you like talking more than writing?

Kinesthetic

- Do you think better when you are moving and walking around?
- Do you gesture a lot while speaking?
- Do you find it hard to sit still?

Auditory People

- talk to themselves while working
- are easily distracted by noise
- move their lips and pronounce the words as they read
- enjoy reading aloud and listening
- can repeat back and mimic tone pitch and timbre
- find writing difficult, but are better at telling
- speak in rhythmic patterns
- are frequently eloquent speakers
- like music more than art
- learn by listening, and remember what was discussed rather than seen
- are talkative, love discussion, and go into lengthy descriptions
- have problems with projects that involve visualization, such as cutting pieces that fit together
- can spell better out loud than in writing
- like jokes better than comics

Kinesthetic People

- speak slowly
- respond to physical rewards
- touch people to get their attention
- stand close when talking to someone
- are physically oriented and move a lot
- have early large-muscle development
- learn by manipulating and doing
- memorize by walking and seeing
- use a finger as a pointer when reading
- gesture a lot
- can't sit still for long periods of time
- can't remember geography unless they've actually been there
- use action words

Understanding both process words and vocal speeds will help you understand others' learning modalities.

Visual

● Common process word in a
conversation:
"The way I *see* it is . . . "

● Vocal speed is quick.

Auditory

● Common process word in a
conversation:
"I *hear* what you're saying."

● Vocal speed is medium.

Kinesthetic

● Common process word in a
conversation:
"I *feel* like you . . . "

● Vocal speed is slower.

- like plot-oriented books — they reflect action with body movement as they read
- may have messy handwriting
- want to act things out
- like involved games

Maybe you know someone who did well in high school but in college started fumbling or even failing classes. This happens to many people, and most of them have no idea what happened to make them start feeling so incompetent. The truth is, there was probably a conflict between the student's preferred learning modality and the teacher's teaching style. This phenomenon is especially prevalent in the switch from high school to college because instruction switches from being highly visual to being mostly auditory. So visual learners, who make up a high percentage of the population, suddenly find that they aren't comprehending as well as they once did.

It's easy to decipher the modalities of other people in your life by noticing what words they use when they are communicating. These words are called predicates, or "process words." When a situation is perceived in someone's mind, it's processed in whatever modality the person prefers; the words and phrases the person uses to describe it reflect that person's personal modality. Once you identify a person's predicates, you can make it a point to match their language when you speak to them. Besides using process words that the person can relate to, you can also match the speed at which he or she talks. Visuals speak quickly, auditories at a medium speed, and kinesthetics more slowly.

Here's a trick you can use during phone conversations. If you're talking to a visual, stand up — it will make you talk faster automatically. If you're talking to a kinesthetic, sit down and put your feet up — it will slow you down. Matching your modality to another's is a great way to create rapport and an atmosphere of

To create rapport when talking on the telephone, talk at the same speed as the person with whom you are speaking.

Visual

People with a visual preference speak quickly. Stand up or sit up straight when you talk with them.

Kinesthetic

People who are kinesthetic learners tend to speak slowly. Lean back. Put your feet up and slow down.

understanding.

Here's a list of common verbal cues by modality:

Visual	Auditory	Kinesthetic
appears to me	all ears	all washed up
bird's-eye view	call on	boils down to
catch a glimpse of	clear as a bell	come to grips with
clear-cut	clearly expressed	floating on thin air
dim view	describe in detail	get a handle on
eye to eye	earful	get a load of this
get a scope on	give me your ear	get in touch with
hazy idea	hear voices	get the drift of
in light of	hidden message	hang in there!
in person	idle talk	hold it!
in view of	loud and clear	hothead
looks like	outspoken	lay cards on table
mental image	rap session	pull some strings
mind's eye	rings a bell	sharp as a tack
pretty as a picture	to tell the truth	slipped my mind
see to it	tuned-in/tuned-out	start from scratch
short-sighted	unheard of	stiff upper lip
showing off	voiced an opinion	too much hassle
tunnel vision	within hearing range	underhanded

Recognizing another person's preferred learning modality is an important key to making your most effective presentation. For instance, if you know your boss is visual, you're much more likely to get your point across if you use visual materials, such as slides and handouts, in a presentation.

How Do You Process Information?

The V-A-K identification system distinguishes how we *perceive* information. To determine brain dominance, or how you *process* information, we use a model first developed by Anthony Gregorc, professor of curriculum and instruction at the University of Connecticut. His investigative studies led him to identify two possibilities of brain dominance:

- concrete and abstract perception, and
- sequential (linear) and random (nonlinear) ordering abilities.

Verbal cues help you to determine a person's learning modality.

Visual

" That *looks* good to me! **"**

Auditory

" That *sounds* good to me! **"**

Kinesthetic

" That *feels* good to me! **"**

These can be combined into four combinations of clustered behaviors that we'll call your thinking style. Gregorc calls these styles *concrete sequential, abstract sequential, concrete random,* and *abstract random.* People who fall into the two "sequential" categories tend to be left-brain dominant, while the "random" thinkers are generally right-brain dominant.

As with V-A-K identification, not everyone can be pigeonholed into one of these classifications. Even so, most of us favor one over the others. Knowing what your dominant style is allows you to "work with it" as well as determine ways to become more balanced.

Think about this: If you were able to control the way you react to a situation and solve a problem by choosing the most effective solution for that particular set of circumstances, how much more successful could you be? In other words, how much more could you achieve if you were "doing the right thing" in most situations?

Different activities demand different types of thinking styles, so it's to your advantage to know, first, which is your predominant style, and second, what you can do to develop the other thinking styles in yourself.

SuperCamp instructor John Parks Le Tellier designed the test at the right to help you identify your personal thinking style or classification. Just read each group of four words, and select the two out of each four that best describe you. There are no right or wrong answers; every person will answer differently. The most important thing is to be honest!

_____

Read each set of words and mark the two that best describe you.

1. a. imaginative
   b. investigative
   c. realistic
   d. analytical

2. a. organized
   b. adaptable
   c. critical
   d. inquisitive

3. a. debating
   b. getting to the point
   c. creating
   d. relating

4. a. personal
   b. practical
   c. academic
   d. adventurous

5. a. precise
   b. flexible
   c. systematic
   d. inventive

6. a. sharing
   b. orderly
   c. sensible
   d. independent

7. a. competitive
   b. perfectionist
   c. cooperative
   d. logical

8. a. intellectual
   b. sensitive
   c. hard-working
   d. risk-taking

9. a. reader
   b. people person
   c. problem solver
   d. planner

10. a. memorize
    b. associate
    c. think-through
    d. originate

11. a. changer
    b. judger
    c. spontaneous
    d. wants directions

12. a. communicating
    b. discovering
    c. cautious
    d. reasoning

13. a. challenging
    b. practicing
    c. caring
    d. examining

14. a. completing work
    b. seeing possibilities
    c. gaining ideas
    d. interpreting

15. a. doing
    b. feeling
    c. thinking
    d. experimenting

After completing the test, circle the letters of the words you chose for each number in the grid below. Add your totals for columns I, II, III, and IV. Multiply the total of each column by 4. The box with the highest number describes how you most often process information.

1.	C	D	A	B
2.	A	C	B	D
3.	B	A	D	C
4.	B	C	A	D
5.	A	C	B	D
6.	B	C	A	D
7.	B	D	C	A
8.	C	A	B	D
9.	D	A	B	C
10.	A	C	B	D
11.	D	B	C	A
12.	C	D	A	B
13.	B	D	C	A
14.	A	C	D	B
15.	A	C	B	D

Total	Total	Total	Total
6	5	12	7
I	II	III	IV

I.	6	x 4 =	24	Concrete Sequential (CS)
II.	5	x 4 =	20	Abstract Sequential (AS)
III.	12	x 4 =	48	Abstract Random (AR)
IV.	7	x 4 =	28	Concrete Random (CR)

Before you read on to discover more about your individual thinking style, look at the graph at the right and chart yourself on it. It's easy — just place a dot on the number that corresponds to your score in each of the classifications, then connect the dots. If you're like most people, you'll see that you actually have some ability in

After you have completed the personal thinking style test, chart your results below.

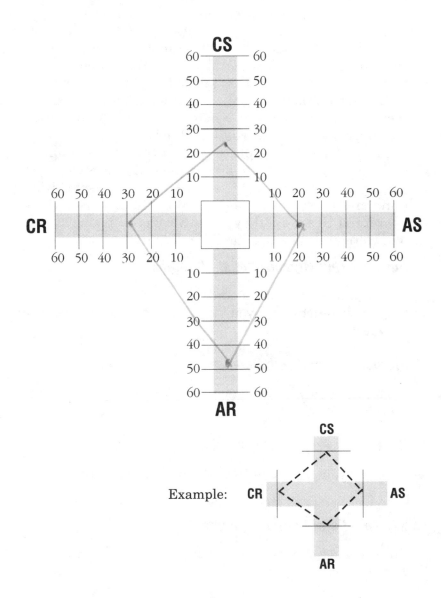

Example:

each of the quadrants. Some people may seem to be rather evenly balanced among them, yet most will obviously favor one and overlap the other three to varying degrees.

Concrete Sequential Thinkers

As the label implies, *concrete sequential* thinkers are based in reality and process information in an ordered, sequential, linear fashion. To CS's, reality consists of what they can detect through their physical senses of sight, touch, sound, taste, and smell. They notice and recall details easily and remember facts, specific information, formulas, and rules with ease. "Hands on" is a good way for these people to learn. CS's need to organize tasks into step-by-step processes and strive for perfection at every step of the way. They like specific directions and procedures. Since most of the business world is ordered this way, they make very good business people. Here are some tips for CS individuals.

Build on Your Organizational Strengths

Organize your days and weeks realistically, planning how much time you need to spend on projects in advance.

Provide Yourself with Details

Make sure you know everything you need to know to complete a task.

Break Your Projects Down into Specific Steps

Give yourself deadlines so you'll know when you're on track.

Set Up a Quiet Work Environment

Know what interferes with your concentration and eliminate it.

Concrete Sequential (CS) thinkers notice and recall details easily, need to organize tasks into step-by-step processes, and strive for perfection.

 ## Tips for CS Thinkers

- Build on your organizational strengths.

- Provide yourself with details.

- Break your projects down into specific steps.

- Set up a quiet work environment.

Concrete Random Thinkers

Concrete random thinkers have an experimental attitude and the less structured behavior that goes along with it. Like concrete sequentials, they're based in reality, but are willing to take more of a trial-and-error approach. Because of this, they often make the intuitive leaps necessary for true creative thought.

They have a strong need to find alternatives and to do things in their own way. Time is not a priority for CR's, and they tend to lose track of it, especially when involved in interesting situations. They're *process* rather than result oriented; consequently, projects seldom turn out the way they were planned because of unexpected possibilities that turn up and invite exploration during the process. Here are some ways for CR people to make the most of their style.

Use Your Divergent Thinking Ability

Believe that it's good to see things from more than one point of view. Come up with alternative ideas and explore them. Create ideas rather than judge them. Keep a questioning attitude.

Set Yourself Up to Solve Problems

Volunteer for projects that involve solving a problem, or work through your own projects by posing a question and then solving it.

Check Your Time

Give yourself deadlines for each step of your task, then resolve to finish it on time!

Accept Your Need for Change

When things start to seem stale, make small changes to keep your mind sharp — even if it just means moving to a new room or area.

Concrete Random (CR) thinkers are based in reality and have an experimental attitude.

 **Tips for CR Thinkers**

- Use your divergent ability.

- Set yourself up to solve problems.

- Check your time.

- Accept your need for change.

- Find personal support.

Find Personal Support

Seek out people who value divergent thinking, for this will help you to feel positive about yourself.

Abstract Random Thinkers

The "real" world for *abstract random* learners is the world of feelings and emotions. They are attuned to nuances and "vibes," and some lean toward mysticism. The AR's mind absorbs ideas, information, and impressions and organizes them through reflection. (Sometimes this takes such a long time that others don't think AR's have much of a reaction or opinion.) They remember best if information is personalized. Feelings can either greatly enhance or interfere with their learning.

They feel constricted when they're subjected to a very structured environment, so you won't find many of them working for insurance companies, banks, or the like. They thrive in unstructured, people-oriented environments.

AR's experience events holistically; they need to see the whole picture at once rather than step by step. For that reason, it's helpful for them to know how things are related to the whole before getting into the details.

Although AR's make up a fair proportion of the population, most of the world doesn't operate in an AR fashion. These thinkers do very well in creative situations and need to work a little harder in more structured situations. Here are some ways for AR people to make the most of their talents.

Use Your Natural Ability to Work with Others

Find colleagues you can work with, and bounce ideas off one another. When you have a task to complete, set deadlines and check in with people often along the way.

Abstract Random (AR) thinkers organize information through reflection and thrive in unstructured, people-oriented environments.

 ## Tips for AR Thinkers

- Use your natural ability to work with others.

- Recognize how strongly emotions influence your concentration.

- Build on your strength of learning by association.

- Look at the big picture.

- Be aware of time.

- Use visual cues.

Recognize How Strongly Emotions Influence Your Concentration

Avoid negative people, and settle personal concerns and problems promptly. These can drain your energy.

Build On Your Strength to Learn by Association

Make visual and verbal associations (see Chapter 9). Use metaphors, silly stories, and other creative expressions to help you remember.

Look at the Big Picture

Work from the large concept to the smaller details.

Be Aware of Time

Be careful to allow enough time to finish the job. Begin with the most difficult task, take a break, then switch to another task. Return to the first task when your mind has cleared. It's okay to work on more than one thing at a time!

Use Visual Cues

Paste stick-on reminder notes in your car, on your bathroom mirror, or wherever you'll be sure to see them. Color code a large monthly calendar with information you need to keep at the front of your mind. Use one color for personal, one for job/career, one for family, and so on.

Abstract Sequential Thinkers

Reality for *abstract sequential* thinkers is the metaphysical world of theory and abstract thought. They like to think in concepts and analyze information. They have a great appreciation for well-organized people and events. It's easy for them to zoom in on what's important, such as key points and significant details. Their

Abstract Sequential (AS) thinkers like to think in concepts and analyze information. They are great philosophers and research scientists.

 ## Tips for AS Thinkers

- Give yourself exercises in logic.

- Feed your intellect.

- Strive for structure.

- Analyze the people you deal with.

thinking processes are logical, rational, and intellectual.

A favorite activity for abstract sequentials is reading, and when a project needs to be researched they are very thorough at it. They want to know the causes behind the effects and to understand theories and concepts. As you can imagine, these people are great philosophers and research scientists. Generally, they prefer to work alone rather than in groups. Here are some tips for AS thinkers.

Give Yourself Exercises in Logic

When problem-solving, turn your problem into a theoretical situation and solve it at that level.

Feed Your Intellect

If you're involved in a project, be sure to read everything you can on the subject so that you'll have all the facts you need to complete it to your standards.

Strive for Structure

In your personal life and career, steer yourself toward highly structured situations. In your projects, chart out the steps and the time involved for each step in advance.

Analyze the People You Deal With

If you know the learning styles of other people it will be easier for you to understand them and make them understand you.

How Different Thinking Styles Would Plan the Same Vacation

Here's an example of how different thinking styles work. If you were a *concrete sequential,* you would tend

A kinesthetic learner overcomes barriers to learning success.

Have you ever suffered through a meeting where a new operation or procedure was introduced, and everyone in the room seemed to grasp it but you? You know most of your coworkers are no more intelligent than you are, so what's the problem? It could be a difference in learning style.

Melissa Roder, of West Hartford, Connecticut, knew what her preferred learning style was, and she was determined to use that knowledge to better her grades. At SuperCamp she took a test that indicated she was a kinesthetic learner. After years of struggling through school, she was thrilled to discover there was nothing wrong with the way she learns; she just learns in a way that hadn't been addressed by many teachers at her grade level.

Back at school, Melissa was anxious to prove to her parents, the school authorities, and especially herself that she had what it takes to make the honor roll. But after two disappointing quarters, she felt confused and stressed. She explained to her guidance counselor that she needed a hands-on learning approach. The school administered twenty-two hours of tests but uncovered no learning disabilities. She was deemed an "enigma."

But she wouldn't give up. She identified those teachers in her school who were also kinesthetic and persuaded the school authorities to put her in those classes. She also asked for and was given a new counselor with whom she had a much better rapport.

By the end of the third quarter of the school year, Melissa had managed to bring her GPA up to 3.0 — and she made the honor roll for the first time ever.

to choose a vacation that you had already taken before: going to the same place, taking the same mode of travel, doing the same activities. You would plan where and when you were going, how long you would stay, how much you would spend. Once you decided, you would specifically plan every step. If you were going someplace you hadn't been before, you would research everything about it that you didn't know. You would write for brochures. You would set up budget categories for hotels, meals, souvenirs, and spending. You might even go so far as to put money in separate envelopes for each purpose.

At the other end of the spectrum, if you were an *abstract random,* you would probably go somewhere that someone told you about and described in glowing terms. You wouldn't make your selection from a brochure. You would have to have a gut feeling about it being a great place to go. You would probably want to take friends along. You would want your vacation to be unstructured, and once you got there, you would do what felt good to do at the moment.

Balancing Your Mind Power

When you know your own thinking style, you can become a more balanced thinker by occasionally forcing yourself to use the thinking and perceiving styles you're less comfortable with. Here are some exercises suggested by Ned Herrmann, an expert on brain dominance, to help develop your less preferred quadrants:

If You're Right-Mode Dominant (AR or CR):

- Find out how a machine you use frequently actually works.
- Organize your photos into albums.
- Be exactly on time all day.
- Develop a personal budget.
- Assemble a model kit by the instructions.

Approaching the planning of vacations can take different paths for different thinking styles.

Concrete Sequentials

- Choose a vacation already taken.

- Plan where and when.

- Decide how long to stay.

- Plan every specific step.

- Write for brochures.

- Set up budget categories for hotels, meals, souvenirs, and spending.

Abstract Randoms

- Go somewhere someone talked about in glowing terms.

- Have a gut feeling about it being a great place to go.

- Take friends along.

- Keep it unstructured.

- Once there, do what feels good to do at that moment.

- Join an investment club.
- Take a current problem and analyze it into main parts.
- Learn to run a personal computer.
- Write a critical review of your favorite movie.
- Organize your books in sequence according to subject.

If You're Left-Mode Dominant (AS or CS):

- Try to understand your pet's feelings.
- Invent a gourmet dish, then prepare it.
- Play with clay and discover its inner meaning.
- Take five hundred photographs without worrying about the cost.
- Create a personal logo.
- Drive to "nowhere" without feeling guilty.
- Play with your children the way they want to play.
- Take a ten-minute "feeling" break every day.
- Play the music you like when you want to hear it.
- Experience your spirituality in a nonreligious way.
- Take a "wrong turn" and explore a new neighborhood.

Want to measure how much you can control your brain dominance? Try doing several of these activities for two to three weeks, then take the test again. Using the chart *on the right,* replot your graph and compare it with the one you did earlier in this chapter. You might be surprised how much change you effected!

Gifted people appear to learn equally well kinesthetically, visually, and auditorily. They are more evenly balanced between right- and left-brain hemispheres. You can improve your ability to learn and to relate to others by developing your least preferred learning modalities.

If you're visual, you can work on your auditory and

Complete any of the suggested activities for two to three weeks, take the test again, replot this graph, and then compare it to your first.

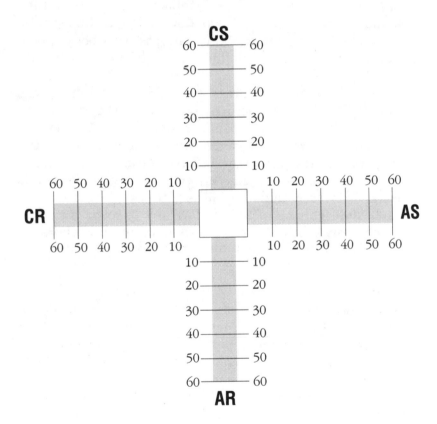

kinesthetic modes by talking through things and acting them out with body movements. For instance, after attending a seminar, tell somebody about it in great detail, using your hands and body to emphasize the high points and important information. (If you can't find anybody who has the time or interest to listen, your pet will no doubt appreciate the attention.)

If you're auditory, wait until after the seminar and make a mindmap (see Chapter 7) of the information you learned, using lots of colors, symbols, and graphics. Like visual people, you can also develop your kinesthetic modes by acting out the key concepts with body movements, or by actually building a model to demonstrate it, if applicable.

As a kinesthetic learner you can also mindmap the material and draw pictures of it (kinesthetics like to draw) to develop your visual mode. Then talk about it out loud, varying your pitch and volume to stress the important parts. Try to speak rhythmically.

Remember, no single thinking style or modality is better or worse than any other; they're just different. Each style can be effective. The key is to be aware of which works best for you, and develop the others as well.

I Know I Know

☑ Check the box if you understand the concept:

☐ I know that I have my own personal learning style.

☐ I know my preferred modality is _____ (visual, auditory, or kinesthetic).

☐ I know I am a _____ thinker (concrete sequential, abstract sequential, abstract random, or concrete random).

☐ I know how to decipher the learning styles of other people.

☐ I know activities for balancing my learning modality and thought process.

☐ I know how to make use of my strongest thought process.

7

Techniques of High-Tech Note-Taking

Why should you read this chapter?

☑ See the whole picture at a glance.

☑ Remember details easily.

☑ See connections between ideas and concepts.

☑ Work with your brain, rather than struggling against it.

☑ Abandon the boring "outline format" forever.

Picture this: You've just come out of an important three-hour planning meeting. For most of that time, you were scribbling notes feverishly, trying to preserve the important points everyone was making. You get back to your desk, open your notes — and just stare. All you see is a bunch of words. Even though your jottings are comprehensive, none of the important points leap out at you. You have bits of what everyone said, but you're not sure how they fit together. It's as if you've got the pieces of a jigsaw puzzle, yet you can't see the whole picture.

What do you do? Embarrass yourself by going back and asking the others to explain what they meant? Take whatever action you can and hope it coincides with the overall plan? Pray for divine guidance?

If you've ever had such a problem, you need this chapter. Here you will discover note-taking techniques that will increase your ability to see the big picture, help you review more efficiently, and enable you to recall more accurately.

Why Take Notes, Anyway?

Effective note-taking is one of the most important skills anyone ever learns. For students, it often means the difference between scoring high or low at test time. For business people, it can mean keeping track of important tasks and projects instead of getting lost in a sea of scattered slips of paper.

The reason for taking notes in the first place is that note-taking enhances recall. The amazing human mind — your mind — stores everything you see, hear, and feel. Your memory is perfect, just like a computer. The trick is not to help the mind remember; it does that automatically. The trick is to help yourself *recall* what's stored in your memory.

Most of us recall best when we *write things down*. Without taking notes and reviewing them, most people are able to recall only a small percentage of material

Check the boxes below if any of the statements sound familiar.

☐ My notepads contain pages and pages of incomprehensible notes.

☐ My desk is cluttered with scraps of paper reminding me to do this or that.

☐ I'm tired of using index cards to organize my speeches and reports.

— If so, read on!

This chapter gives you step-by-step directions for two note-taking methods that will help you eliminate the negatives checked above.

they heard or read as recently as the day before. Effective note-taking saves time by helping you file information easily and recall it on demand.

"Mental notes" don't work because the brain focuses on whatever is vying for its attention at a particular moment. And even when we do remember a "mental note," it often comes back to us in the same fuzzy, haphazard way we stored it in our brains originally. So if you want to remember something — if you *have* to remember it — write it down.

But what exactly should we write down? How *much* should we write, and in what format? Should we take notes in a traditional outline form, a summary, or maybe a series of statements? What should good notes look like?

The Not-So-Good, Old-Fashioned Outline Format

Most of us were taught at some time to take notes using an outline format, similar to the notes at right. This style was taught to many of us by teachers who outlined their notes or lectures and simply figured that if they taught in outline form, we should learn in outline form. The trouble is, even when teachers work from an outline, they rarely deliver the material in the same way. They forget things and backtrack. They digress. Someone asks a question, and the teacher answers it, often including important material that wasn't in the outline at all.

When a speaker backtracks to something she forgot, you've got to find a way to fit that information into your nice, neat format. Instead of taking effective notes and really understanding what's being presented, you end up losing the substance of it in the "form" of your note-taking. The traditional outline style also makes it tough to get an overview and see connections between ideas. Furthermore, reviewing outlined notes is so boring, you're tempted to just skip it all together.

Traditional outline note-taking forms are usually difficult to follow and rarely present the "true" substance of the subject matter.

```
Beowulf
I. Background information
    A. History
        1. Oldest epic poem written in English
        2. Composed in the 8th century
        3. Only existing manuscript damaged in a
           fire in 1731, many lines and words of
           poem lost

    B. Language
        1. Written in Old English (Anglo-Saxon)
        2. Alliterative meter - alliteration is
           principal organizing device

            a) Each line is divided into two half
               lines, with four strong stresses per
               line
            b) Stressed syllables in first
               half-line alliterate with stressed
               syllables of second half line
            c) Example: "In a somer seson, whan
               soft was the sonne"
               (Piers Plowman)

II. Text
    A. Plot
        1. Poem is about two Scandinavian tribes,
           the Danes and the Geats
        2. Beowulf - hero of story, warrior
        3. Beowulf fights three monsters: Grendal,
           Grendal's mother, and dragon
        4. Monsters represent distortion of social
           form, associated with social evil

            a) Eat people
            b) Don't pay feudal money to kings
```

Working as the Brain Works

Your main objective in note-taking is to *get the key points* from books, reports, lectures, whatever. Good, effective notes help you to remember details about the key points, understand major concepts, and see relationships among them.

Recent research on how the brain stores and recalls information has resulted in new note-taking techniques that make it possible for you to be better organized, increase your understanding, retain information longer, and gain new insight.

Until recently, it was thought that our brains processed information linearly — that is, in a structured, ordered format, like a list. We assumed this because the two most conscious forms of human communication are both linear — speech and print. But that's because physical limitations require that our mouths form only one word at a time. And if we want others to understand us, those words need to be in some sort of order, rather than just a jumble of sounds. Now, however, scientists recognize that this is the "outcome," not the "process" of communication. In fact, the process the mind goes through before it produces those linear speech patterns is anything but linear.

For us to communicate with words, our brains must simultaneously search, sort, select, formulate, order, organize, link, and make sense of a mixture of preconscious words and ideas. At the same time, these words are interwoven with pictures, symbols, images, sounds, and feelings. So what we have is a marvelous jumble that bounces furiously around in the brain but comes out one word at a time, connected by logic, ordered by grammar, and making pretty good sense.

That's what happens on the communicator's end — in the brain of the person who's talking. The same kind of thing happens for the people hearing those words. Although they hear them one at a time, understanding

Linear communication requires the mind to sort through bits of diverse, random, and chaotic information.

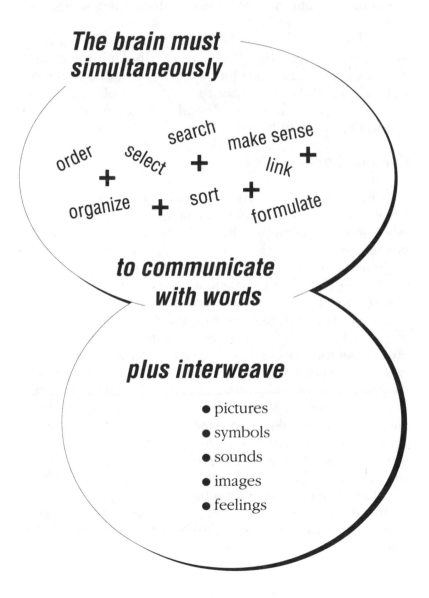

The brain must simultaneously

order + select + search + make sense +

organize + sort + link

+ formulate

to communicate with words

plus interweave

- pictures
- symbols
- sounds
- images
- feelings

them is a complex matter. Listeners must define each word in the context of the words before and after it. Then, based on their own perceptions, experiences, and biases, they must interpret what the words mean.

Research into this complex process of communication has resulted in a reevaluation of how textbooks are written, how effective teaching is done, and how effective notes are taken.

Following are two note-taking techniques that I have found to be especially effective — Mind Mapping and Notes:TM (which stands for Notes: Taking and Making). Both styles can enable you to see the whole picture at one glance and make the mental connections that help you understand and remember.

Mind Mapping™

This is a whole-brain approach that lets you fit an entire subject on one page. By using visual images and other graphic devices, Mind Mapping makes a deeper impression.

This technique of note-taking was developed in the early 1970s by Tony Buzan and is based on the previously mentioned research on how the brain actually works. Your brain often recalls information in the form of pictures, symbols, sounds, shapes, and feelings. A Mind Map uses these visual and sensory reminders in a pattern of connected ideas, like a road map to use for studying, organizing, and planning. It can generate original ideas and easy recall. It's easier than traditional methods of note-taking because it activates both sides of your brain (thus the term "whole-brain approach"). It's also relaxing, fun, and creative. Your mind will never balk at the thought of reviewing your notes when they're in the form of Mind Maps!

Take a moment and look at the page to the right. Close your eyes and picture an apple on that page. (Do this now.)

Mind Mapping is a whole-brain technique using visual images and other graphic devices to form impressions.

Close your eyes and imagine an apple on this page.

Where did you picture the apple on the page? In the upper right corner? Lower left? In the center? Was your picture black-and-white or color?

Most people will picture things in the center of the page and in color. That's how the brain stores information. Naturally, the best notes work *with* your brain rather than against it.

Now look at the Mind Map at the right. (It's a Mind Map of notes about Mind Mapping.) Study it for a minute.

Now, test yourself. Look away or cover it up and ask yourself the following questions:

- What are the titles of the four main branches?
- Where does the bottom arrow point to?
- What symbols are on the upper left branches?
- What are three tips for better Mind Maps?

You may amaze yourself by remembering all or most of these things — even if you've always considered yourself poor at noticing details. It's easy to remember details from a Mind Map because it's written in a form that your brain naturally follows.

Mind Maps are particularly good for planning and organizing things. Remember the planning meeting we discussed at the beginning of this chapter? You could have made the entire meeting more effective if you had Mind Mapped the agenda *beforehand,* then used your Mind Map as a guide in following what everyone had to say. Details could have been filled in as the meeting went along — and you wouldn't have needed to scribble so furiously for three hours.

How to Make a Mind Map

To make a Mind Map, use colored pens and start in the middle of your paper. If it's convenient, turn the

Details from a Mind Map are easy to remember because they follow the brain's pattern of thought.

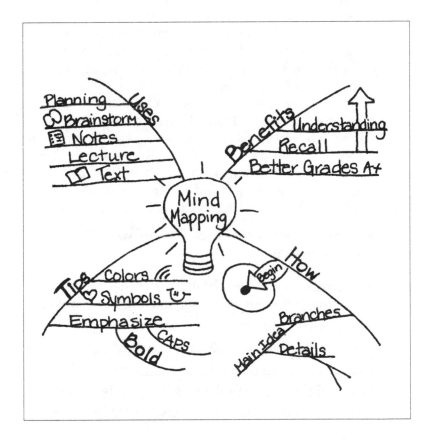

paper sideways to provide more space. Then follow these steps:

1. Print the main topic or idea in the middle of the paper and enclose it in a circle, square, or other shape. For instance, my Mind Map is enclosed in a light bulb.
2. Add a branch extending out from the center for each key point or main idea. The number of branches will vary with the number of ideas or segments. Use a different color for each branch. (In this book, we don't have the advantage of color, so just imagine it.)
3. Write a key word or phrase on each branch, building out to add details. Key words are those that convey the heart of an idea and trigger your memory. If you use abbreviations, be sure you're familiar with them so you'll instantly be able to identify what they stand for days or weeks later.
4. Add symbols and illustrations for better recall.

Here are some ways you can make your Mind Map notes more memorable.

-   Write legibly, or print, using CAPITAL letters.
-   Make important ideas larger so they will jump out at you when you read back over your notes.
-   Personalize your Mind Map with things that relate to you. The symbol of a clock might mean this item has an important deadline. Some people use arrows to point to "action items," or things they must act on.
-   Underline words. Use **bold** letters.
-   Be creative and outrageous in your design, because the brain remembers the unusual more easily.
-   Use random shapes to point out certain items or ideas.

Tips to Make a Mind Map

- In the middle of the paper, enclose the main idea.

- Add a branch from the center for each key point — use colors.

- Write a key word/phrase on each branch, building out to add details.

- Add symbols and illustrations.

- Use legible CAPITAL letters.

- Make important ideas larger.

- Personalize your Mind Map.

- <u>Underline</u> words and use **bold** letters.

- Be creative and outrageous.

- Use random shapes to point out items or ideas.

- Construct Mind Maps horizontally.

- Construct your Mind Map horizontally to increase the amount of room you have for your work.

Additional Tips

To summarize information from nonfiction books, branches can be given the same titles as the boldface print or chapter headings in the text. Subheadings throughout the chapters can also provide branches that are meaningful. If you're like me, you often read a book with hopes of learning some specific information. Take time to preview the book before you actually read it, and make a Mind Map of the points you hope to learn about. Then fill in the branches as you read.

If you're at a loss for a way to organize your notes for, let's say, that planning meeting we've been talking about, just put "Planning Meeting" in the center and label each branch with the name of a person who's giving a report at the meeting. Then each report can flow from an individual branch.

Some people like to redo their Mind Maps later as a review. Reviewing information within twenty-four hours of hearing it is an important key to retention. Other people like to take notes in a different form during a speech or lecture, then Mind Map them later. One man I know is a police officer who takes notes in Mind Map form when he's interviewing a witness, then uses those notes when filling out the linear, logical forms required by his department.

In addition to being an effective method of note-taking, Mind Mapping works well for other tasks. It's ideal for writing and remembering presentations you have to make, because you can fit an entire speech onto one page. Just a glance at your sheet of paper will remind you of your next topic of discussion, with key words provided to prompt your memory. It works equally well for reports or term papers, though you may need to use more than one map for topics with many

Creating Mind Maps horizontally increases the amount of room you have for your work, like the speech below.

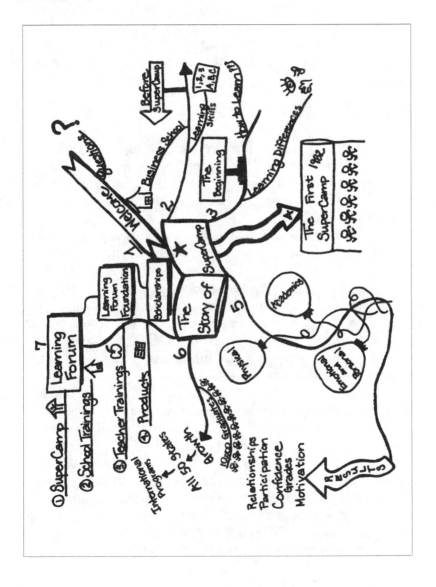

details. I've even used Mind Maps for letter- and memo-writing and for telephone conversations, just to be sure I don't forget anything important.

For a more complete look at Mind Mapping and its uses for everything from note-taking to brainstorming and from project management to personal growth, see Joyce Wycoff's book *Mindmapping: Your Personal Guide to Exploring Creativity and Problem-Solving* (New York; Berkley Books, 1991). This book not only gives excellent background on understanding the brain and creativity, it also describes in detail the many applications of Mind Mapping.

Notes:TM

Notes:TM is short for "Notes: Taking and Making." The most important feature of this system is that it allows you to record your personal thoughts and conclusions *along with* the key parts of a speech or reading material.

In order to learn Notes:TM, you'll want to understand the distinction between Note-*Taking* and Note-*Making*. Note-*Taking* involves listening to what a speaker or teacher is saying and writing down the key points as you go. Note-*Making* involves writing down your *own* thoughts and impressions as you listen to the material being presented. Notes:TM lets you do both things at once — record the information and keep track of your own thoughts.

Notes:TM is a way of applying both our conscious and subconscious minds to the same material *in a purposeful way*. Actually, both minds are at work no matter what note-taking method we use. While our conscious minds are intently focusing on the material and the process of getting it down on paper, our subconscious minds are reacting, forming impressions, making connections, and doing a whole host of things more or less automatically. Notes:TM coordinates both of these mental activities to achieve a more effective result.

Notes:TM applies both the conscious and subconscious minds to the material at hand.

Date

Location

Topic

Thoughts

Impressions

Feelings

Reactions

Questions

Concerns

How to Use Notes:TM

Start with a sheet of paper (lined or unlined, which-ever you prefer) and draw a line vertically, about one-third of the way in from the right edge. The left side of the paper is for *taking* notes; the right side (the smaller space) is for *making* notes.

On the left side, write what the speaker is saying — key points, terms, diagrams, and figures. On the right, record your own thoughts, feelings, reactions, questions, and concerns, pretty much as they come up. On the note-taking side, limit yourself to the information that's coming to you from the outside. On the note-making side, write whatever comes to mind, without censoring it. Your note-making might come out thus:

"This is incredible. . . . This is boring. . . . I'm not fol-lowing this. . . . Where did he just go? . . . I know how I can use this in another situation. . . . How does this relate to what he said earlier? . . . "

Writing down your thoughts in this way helps you focus your concentration and bring your attention back to what the speaker is saying. Later, it can help you bet-ter understand the notes you took, remind you of things you want to cross-check, spur you to make phone calls, or just pick out the items that had the biggest impact on you when you were hearing them.

Mark Reardon, director of training for SuperCamp, made use of the Notes:TM technique when he heard a speech by Randolph Craft about the late Buckminster Fuller. The presentation included a video of Fuller. Reardon recalls, "As I listened to him speak, I noticed that at the beginning he was not saying anything I needed to write down or remember specifically. He was using this time to set us up for what he was planning to talk about later.

"So, as he spoke, I wrote down my physical observa-tions about him on the note-making section of my paper . . . the way he held his hands, the way his face looked.

By practicing Notes:TM, Mark Reardon recalls specific ideas and thoughts from a presentation he attended.

Randolf Craft
on Buckminster Fuller

5·26·91
Kona, HI

Background experience with B.F. and the video project	I'm interested to know more about Bucky☺
"Facilitated Video" • able to ask questions "at the moment" so • learning can be Maximized	It will be interesting to get a sense of Bucky's magic * I like this concept
└ Ron Hubbard Learning stops as soon as you don't understand one word ☹	I never thought of that happening before
Video Presentation • Influence of Grandmother "Golden Rule"	B. sitting... bald, silver glasses, "old voice"
* Working for everyone makes you more effective!	Wow! Service is the issue! ☺

Now, when I review my notes of that speech, these comments bring up emotions and feelings in me and I can hear his voice in my head."

When using the Notes:TM technique, take a minute or two after the speech or lecture to go back over your notes and add your own personal graphics — symbols and pictures that are meaningful to you. It's best to make up your own symbols, but here are some ideas to help you get started:

> ! = important point
> arrow = connection to something else on the page
> smiley face = positive
> sad face = negative
> 3X = repeated 3 times (must be important!)

The symbols can mean whatever you want them to. However, stay with the same symbols and meanings once you have a system.

When you review your notes, the symbols trigger your mind to remember what the speaker was saying as well as relive what you were thinking at the time, consciously and subconsciously. Often, the most valuable thing we get from a meeting, speech, or lecture is not the material itself but the ideas it sparks in our minds.

I've found that the Notes:TM technique works best for taking notes during a speech, meeting, or seminar. It can also work well for taking notes on reading material. The principle and the process are much the same. The major difference is that when you're reading, you're going at your own pace and you don't have to worry that your note-*making* is causing you to miss any of the material you're getting in your note-*taking*.

Practice Makes Permanent

Like any new technique, both of these systems take practice before they become a permanent part of your information-gathering system. A new way of note-taking

Symbols trigger ideas, recall the speaker's comments, and help to bring back thoughts about the presentation.

! = important point

⋮ = connections

☺ = positive

☹ = negative

3x = repeated 3 times

can feel strange and awkward. You may not feel sure that you are getting the information you need, and you may want to revert to the old "known" methods — something that has worked okay for you in the past. But give it a chance. What do you have to lose? With your old system, how much do you remember an hour after hearing something? How much can you reconstruct a day, a week, or a month later?

Remember, it takes commitment to use a new skill long enough for it to become familiar. When I first learned how to Mind Map, I was frustrated. I didn't understand how I was going to remember all the information I needed to know based on the little scribbles I was writing. It seemed so inadequate, compared with the volumes of outlined notes I used to amass.

But I was in a class and committed to a week of Mind Mapping throughout each day. I Mind Mapped during lectures, I took ideas and Mind Mapped them, I Mind Mapped things I was reading, and so it went. Something happened to me during this process; I discovered I was remembering more. Ideas were clearer to me. The very process of preserving those ideas was more fun and interesting. I was more involved with what was being said. Finally, I trusted the technique — and I've been using it ever since. Practice made it permanent for me. And it can for you.

More Note-Taking Tips

Regardless of which method you use, here are some tips that can help you take more effective notes:

Listen Actively

Ask yourself, "What does the speaker expect me to learn? Why? What is he saying? How does it relate to the subject? Is it important? Is it something I need to be sure to remember"? Asking these questions makes it easier to select and separate what is important from

Tips to Note-Taking

■ Listen actively.

■ Observe actively.

■ Participate.

■ Preview.

■ Make the auditory visual.

■ Make reviewing easy.

■ Commit to giving it a chance.

what is unimportant. If you use the Notes:TM technique, this provides you with a steady supply of things to jot down on the right side of the line.

Always summarize important and meaningful information and ideas that you need to retain, remember, and use. Notes should focus on material that's important or will be needed later.

Observe Actively

Pay attention to clues you can pick up from the speaker and your reading material. Clues in the reading material can take the form of headings, bold type, italics, pictures, graphs, and diagrams. Some books have chapter outlines that contain important topics. Look at section and chapter summaries. Note the author's or speaker's conclusions. Look for physical clues from the speaker too. Every speaker has a unique style; you can pick up on important points by becoming familiar with that style. Activate your antennae to the speaker's facial expressions, gestures, body movements, and raised or lowered voice. Notice when she repeats an idea or word, and be attentive to what she writes on the board. Always sit as close to the front of the room as possible — it's easier to pick up on important clues that way.

Participate

If you don't understand something or have a question about it, ask. Join in discussions. Some people hold back, worrying about what others might think. Surveys show that people in an audience usually think highly of participators, often envying them for their courage even when they resent them for interrupting. Besides, what's the worst other people can think — that you're selfish in wanting to gain new knowledge?

Successful note-taking brings recognition.

Sarah Singer of Canton, Ohio, was surprised at how much attention her Mind Mapping skills brought her. At first, her history teacher was put off by the strange doodles Sarah was constantly making in class, but he told her, "You do well in my class, so I can't complain. But, frankly, I don't understand how you do it." So she explained what she was doing and talked about how the brain stores information.

Sarah's psychology teacher learned about her technique from the history teacher and asked her to teach Mind Mapping to the psych class. On the day she demonstrated it for the class, several other teachers sat in to listen. Eventually, the school principal found out about Sarah's technique and asked her to teach a whole day of classes — and she's done so every year since then.

Now a senior at Ohio State's College of Education, Sarah still uses Mind Mapping in her classes. She's given many presentations at the university and has gotten many of her fellow students involved with the technique as well.

Preview

If you know what a speaker or lecturer is going to discuss, preview the material and find as much information on it as possible beforehand. Having some knowledge ahead of time will help you identify important points during a speech or lecture.

You'll also know which concepts are unclear to you, so you can be prepared to ask questions. As you hear bits of information, you'll find it easier to see how they fit together in the big picture. Previewing is one of the most effective ways to insure success and understanding.

I know you're thinking, "Who has time to preview?" The answer to that is, previewing actually takes very little time. Often just a few moments scanning an agenda or looking over notes from a previous meeting is all you'll need to do. All your mind needs is a little stimulation.

Make the Auditory Visual

Your notes should be personal and meaningful to you, just like snapshots. Have you ever noticed how a snapshot from a vacation or important event brings a flood of memories — things you thought you'd forgotten?

When you're taking in information, snap pictures of it by adding visual associations like symbols, drawings, and arrows as they occur to you. This way, your notes, even if reviewed months later, will remind you instantly of the material you knew was important at the time — and need to recall now.

Make Reviewing Easy

When taking/making notes, write on only one side of the paper. Use single sheets, not paper in a bound notebook. Then you can lay the sheets out in front of you or hang them up on the wall later, when you need to review.

A creative use of Mind Mapping helps with goals.

Dear Fellow Mind Mappers:

I have an idea I thought you might find useful. Last year, I found myself without a good calendar for the new year, so I grabbed a school calendar and stuck it on my wall. It was quite boring, featuring the stereotypical stilted pictures of all the department heads. So I took it down, covered that one month's picture with blank paper, and made a colorful Mind Map of everything I wanted to accomplish that month. It was a positive, supporting reminder that I couldn't help but look at every day.

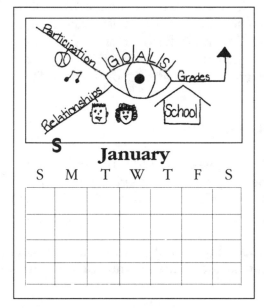

For me, this calendar now is a symbol of strength — not just physical, but inner strength. This means "going for it!" — putting myself out of my comfort zone and taking 100 percent risk, knowing that I am strong enough to handle any situation and that I can always count on myself.

The eye in the calendar symbolizes sight — not just being able to see, but being able to "see through" a situation, knowing clearly what my goals are and exactly what I want the outcome to be. Sight also involves seeing things in myself: Am I putting on an act? Or is this really me? It also means being able to see everything around me in a positive light.

Sincerely,

Gary Cohen

Copy key notes on three-by-five cards that you can carry around with you. When you're standing in line, riding a bus, or waiting for an appointment, you can take them out for a few minutes of extra study or thinking time.

C'mon, Try It

I invite you to commit to a period of time to try these note-taking skills. No matter what your learning style, I encourage you to use and practice both techniques in various situations. You may discover that you want to use both methods, each in a different situation. Or you may discover that you have a strong preference for one or the other.

Benefits of Mind Mapping

It's Flexible. If a speaker suddenly remembers to make a point about a previous thought, you can easily add it to the appropriate place on your Mind Map without creating confusion.

It Focuses Attention. You're not concerned with catching every word that is said. Instead, you can concentrate on ideas.

It Increases Understanding. When reading a text or technical report, Mind Mapping increases understanding and provides great review notes for later.

It's Fun. Your imagination and creativity are limitless, and that makes taking and reviewing notes more fun.

Benefits of Notes:TM

It's Easier To Remember a subject when you read what you were thinking about at the time.

Benefits of Mind Mapping

■ It's flexible.

■ It focuses attention.

■ It increases understanding.

■ It's fun.

Benefits of Notes:TM

■ It's easier to remember a subject.

■ It focuses your emotions.

■ It's constructive daydreaming.

■ It records your judgments.

It Focuses Your Emotions and helps you tap into your emotional memory.

It's Constructive Daydreaming. It occupies your mind and makes you aware of your thoughts and of where they are drifting, so you can bring them back and stay more in control. (This helps you when you feel the speaker isn't talking fast enough or saying enough to keep your interest.)

It Records Your Judgments, making you more aware of them so you can be more open to seeing another side. It's especially helpful to write down when you disagree with the speaker or don't believe what the speaker is saying. You can say to yourself, "I may disagree, but I can listen and keep an open mind while he is speaking."

I Know I Know

✓ Check the box if you understand the concept:

☐ I know two whole-brain ways to take notes:

1 _____

2 _____

☐ I know how to make my notes memorable.

☐ I know three benefits of Mind Mapping:

1 _____

2 _____

3 _____

☐ I know three benefits of Notes:TM:

1 _____

2 _____

3 _____

☐ I know I can commit to using these methods

for _____ (time period).

8

Write with Confidence

Why should you read this chapter?

☑ Discover fast and easy brainstorming techniques.

☑ Create vivid languaging using your own style and voice.

☑ Take writing projects from start to finish with little stress.

☑ Look forward to writing!

Believe it or not, we are all writers. Somewhere at the core of every human being is a unique and talented soul that gets deep satisfation from telling a story, explaining how to do something, or just sharing thoughts and feelings. We are as driven to write as we are to talk; to communicate our thoughts and experiences to other people; to give them a little taste of who we are.

Children are natural, uninhibited writers who always have something to say. Often what they write is so fresh and profound, it makes folks around them see things in ways they never did before. You may feel far removed from this child who can spill words onto a page with only a moment's thought, but somewhere inside you lives that childlike writer you used to be.

As children, our minds bubble over with ideas, and we never stop to think our ideas might be stupid — that is, until we reach a certain point in our schooling. Then something happens to stop the natural flow of our creativity. Self-consciousness sets in. We become critical of ourselves, ensnared in a mind-gripping struggle with our thoughts every time we sit down to do any formal writing. It's like finding ourselves in a maze where we come up against so many dead ends that eventually we're overcome with frustration and just sit down and sulk — or turn away from the game completely and do something else.

This battle is a result of formal teaching techniques that turn writing into a mostly left-brain process. Instead of allowing a flow of imagination and expression, the process bogs us down in planning and outlines, grammar and punctuation, structuring and editing. Traditional teaching techniques ignore the truth: that writing is a whole-brain activity. In fact, though the complete process involves both sides of the brain in a variety of ways, the role of the right brain has to come first. The right hemisphere is where novelty, fire, and emotion originate. If we skip the step of calling upon our

Writing is a whole-brain activity which accesses the right (emotional) and left (logical) sides.

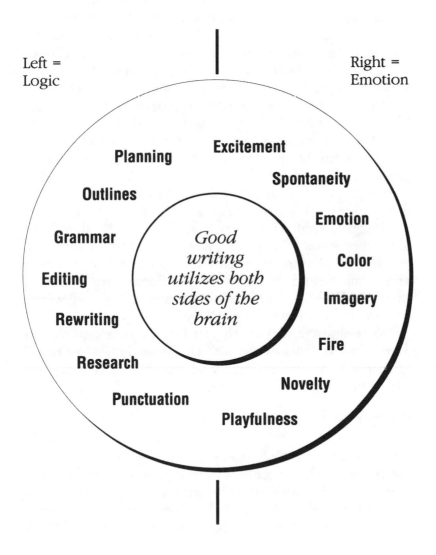

Left =
Logic

Right =
Emotion

Planning

Excitement

Spontaneity

Outlines

Emotion

Grammar

Good writing utilizes both sides of the brain

Color

Editing

Imagery

Rewriting

Fire

Research

Novelty

Punctuation

Playfulness

right-brain energy, we can't even get started. We have no fuel to propel us. This lack of fuel has come to be known as writer's block.

Mark Twain said, "If we taught our children to speak in the way we teach them to write, most of us would t-t-talk l-l-like th-th-this." When most of us were going through school, writing was still being taught as it had been in Twain's time. Today, many children are fortunate to be taught using methods that embrace their right-brain creativity. As adult writers, the first thing we need to learn is how to get back to the unselfconscious "storytelling mode" of our childhood. We need ways of unleashing our creative thought processes.

Imagine that your mind is a reservoir of hot ideas, bubbling and boiling, straining to be set free. The dam that holds them back is writer's block. So strong is this dam, it actually prevents you from putting your pen to paper and starting to write. But don't become discouraged. Just because the thoughts aren't flowing doesn't mean they aren't there!

Imagine that a tiny crack appears in the dam, and ideas begin to trickle out, slowly at first. There's so much force behind the trickle that the crack gets bigger and bigger, and soon those hot ideas are spurting through. Finally the dam bursts and a flood of words rushes out — a river of creativity!

This chapter will teach you two ways to "break the dam." One is "clustering" and the other is "fastwriting." Both methods are extremely effective, and they're also lots of fun. So let's learn them.

Clustering

Developed by Gabriele Rico, clustering is a way of sorting through a jumble of related thoughts and getting them down on paper quickly, without judging their correctness or value. A cluster takes form on paper much as a thought process occurs in your brain, though

Clustering is a way of sorting through ideas and putting them on paper quickly, without judgment.

■ *See and make* connections between ideas.

■ *Expand* on ideas already presented.

■ *Trace* the brain's path taken to arrive at a concept.

■ *Work* naturally with ideas without editing or judgment.

■ *Visualize* specific pieces and recall them with ease.

■ *Experience* the sudden urge to write. At SuperCamp we call it an "aha!"

greatly simplified. The cluster is a free-flowing, organic-looking structure similar to the diagram of a molecule you saw in high school chemistry.

As you experiment with clustering, you'll notice it has distinct similarities to mindmapping. Both are based on the same theory of the brain, which means they both work for the same reasons. Both techniques provide several advantages:

- they allow you to see and make connections between ideas;
- they help you expand on ideas already presented; and
- they enable you to trace the path your brain took to arrive at a particular concept.

To see how clustering works, try this. Write the word *circle* in the center of a blank, unlined piece of paper, then circle it. Now, jot down all the associations you can make to the word *circle*, clustering them around the center word. Circle each new word or phrase and connect it to the center word.

You may find that one of your secondary words prompts a new association. For instance, if the word *circle* makes you think of spinning, spinning may make you think of somersaults and cartwheels. If one association triggers a chain of other associations, stay with it, and write down all the thoughts it triggers, even if they seem unrelated. Then go back to the word *circle* and continue to write down everything you think of. Don't worry how it will all fit together. Take four to five minutes to do this now. When you've finished, look at your cluster and notice all the ideas that that one word generated.

If you were using the clustering technique to stimulate ideas for a real writing project, you would want to notice any patterns that would give you a starting point for what you planned to write.

This technique is powerful because it allows you to work naturally with ideas without editing any of them as you go. If you're like most people, many of your ideas

In clustering, all thoughts are ranked equally, creating a chain reaction of creativity.

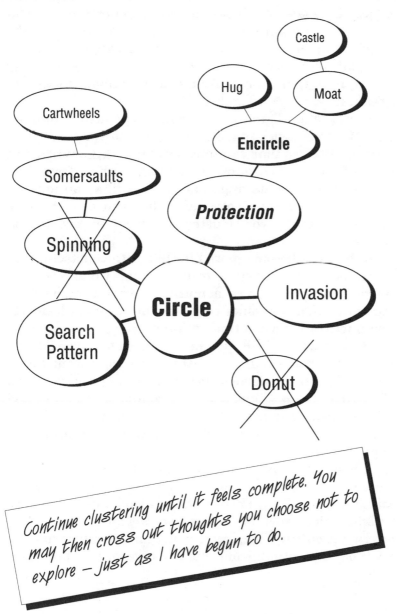

Continue clustering until it feels complete. You may then cross out thoughts you choose not to explore – just as I have begun to do.

never reach paper because you believe they aren't good enough or aren't related to whatever topic you happen to be working on. In clustering, you rank each thought equally with every other thought. When you accept all ideas, even if they don't immediately make sense, you allow your brain to continue producing ideas. When you stop to evaluate, you block the creative process. A seemingly inferior or off-the-wall association is frequently the spark that sets off a brilliant chain reaction of ideas. If you edit your ideas at this stage, you may be snuffing out a real brainstorm. And remember, *all* ideas are great ideas (at least potentially).

Now, take all the ideas from your cluster, number them in a sequence that seems logical to you, and begin writing. Realize that your cluster is only a starting point and that as you write, other ideas will spring forth. The key is flexibility. Staying flexible will allow you to write without overediting. Notice also that you don't have to use everything on your cluster — just the ideas you wish to use.

When you become more familiar with this technique, you'll begin to notice a peculiar and wondrous phenomenon: There comes a point, as you work on your cluster, when you suddenly feel an urgent desire to begin writing. We call this an "aha!"

To experience this phemomenon right now, I'd like you to do another cluster — this time using your favorite color. Keep clustering until you feel the urge to write. Though it takes some people a couple of minutes and others somewhat longer, everybody reaches the "aha!" eventually. When you get there, stop clustering and begin writing.

Clustering can be done on a single word such as *circle, red,* or *life,* and on dichotomies such as *men / women, love / hate,* or *always / never.* It can also be used for more complex ideas such as *western movement, customer service,* or *local area networks.* You can use clustering for all types of writing, from reports, essays, and proposals

An "aha" is reached when writing suddenly takes immediate priority over clustering.

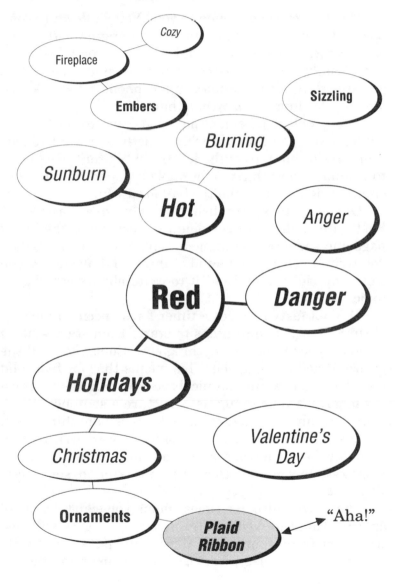

to poetry and stories. Try it for all of these and others as well. You'll find that the resulting writing is coherent and has a natural flow.

Fastwriting

Has this ever happened to you? You sit down to compose a letter or a memo. But like an engine with a bad carburetor, you experience false start after false start, until finally you get frustrated and just put it aside. You go through the mail, or make a few phone calls, or knock off early for lunch — *anything* but write.

The problem is, sometimes you have to write for a while before you find out what exactly you want to say. You have to jump past the left-brain "editor" who wants to evaluate everything before it's on paper, and let your creative right brain take the ball for a while.

One way to accomplish this is with a "fastwrite." Fastwrites help you overcome the obstacle of the blank page and see progress immediately. You can do it before you write to clear your mind of internal dialogue, or you can jump right in and use it to write about your chosen topic.

To do a fastwrite, set a timer for a specified amount of time — say, five minutes to start. Then start writing — about your topic, or anything else. Continue until the entire period has elapsed. This means that for five solid minutes you'll write as quickly as you can, never pausing to gather your thoughts, structure a sentence, check your grammar, backtrack, or cross anything out. Because of the nature of this process, your writing will probably be somewhat scattered and contain spelling mistakes, incomplete thoughts, and run-on sentences. *That's okay.*

There will also be times when you can't think of another thing to write, or your aching fingers will distract you from your topic. If that happens, just write "what else what else what else," or "ow my hand hurts,"

Overcoming the obstacle of the blank page, fastwriting provides visible and immediate progress.

1. Choose a subject.

2. Set timer for a specified amount of time.

3. Start writing continuously, even if what you write is —
"I can't think of what to write!"

4. While the timer is on, avoid:
- Gathering thoughts
- Structuring sentences
- Checking grammar
- Backtracking
- Crossing anything out.

5. Continue until the timer goes off and it's time to stop.

or whatever words come flowing from your brain, until your topic comes back to mind.

On the page to the right is an example of a fastwrite. Now do a fastwrite of your own on your favorite color. Set your timer for five minutes, and begin.

As you look back over your fastwrite, you'll notice that a lot of it seems like pure rubbish, while some of it has a touch of clarity and truth. Realize that you're not going to keep all the things you wrote here. Later, you'll use your fastwrite material as the basis for your finished document, pulling out usable ideas and organizing them. The important thing is not trying to "get it right" the first time. That rarely happens anyway. Even the best writers start out with imperfect drafts. With a fastwrite, you *plan* on not getting it right the first time. This releases you from the pressure to perform and frees you to begin setting out the thoughts and ideas that will eventually become the sentences and paragraphs of your letter or report.

To get used to this process, do fastwrites for increasing periods of time. Begin with five minutes, move on to seven, then ten, twelve, fifteen, and twenty minutes. For a very involved, complex subject, you might even need to fastwrite for as long as forty-five minutes. Fastwriting clears your mind, focuses your ideas, and makes the invisible *visible*.

Show Not Tell

Think about examples of writing that really "pulled you in" — the first few paragraphs of a mystery novel, a very personal, very intimate letter, an impassioned political essay. What was it about the writing that was so gripping? Regardless of the type of writing it was, chances are the reason you were so impressed was that the words caused pictures to form in your mind and feel-

Fastwriting provides opportunities to choose writing gems and turn them into golden pieces.

Red.   *Red is a hot color, a fast color. Red is a color that looks vogue on some people and tacky on others. I like red. I like red ornaments on Christmas trees. I like red hearts on Valentine's Day, and red, plaid ribbon. It is a color that demands respect, even when you draw with red, it needs to have its own space and can't be blended with others colors. Red is a signal for danger and stop. Red is also a color for anger or passion. Red means business. Red roses and red wine are stronger than white roses or white wine. Red is a cheerful color, bright and simple. Red can also be a scary color. Red is the color of blood. Red is a good eye-catcher. My hand is getting cramped. Don't stop. Keep going. Write about red. I enjoy the way red stands out. Red brings strong memories to most people. Memories of red wagons and red sleds, red apples in your lunchbox, red scarves, red mittens. Red stripes on a marine's uniform means he is at least a corporal. Red stripes on the flag signify the blood of men who fought in the revolution. Red is spicy. Red sometimes means cherry-flavored, sometimes cinnamon-flavored. Red is simply red.*

ings to rise in your gut. For instance, if you're reading a charity mailer, you're much more likely to reach for your checkbook if, rather than saying, "There's a famine in Africa," the mailer describes in detail what it looks, feels, and sounds like when tiny, helpless children starve to death.

Vivid descriptions are powerful tools for writers. When you learn to write descriptions, you'll be able to develop visual pictures in readers' minds. You'll transform dry statements of fact into fascinating illustrations. People will not only read and understand, they'll relate and *react*.

One of the best ways to learn to do this is called "Show Not Tell." Developed by Rebekah Caplan, this technique takes "telling sentences" and converts them to "showing paragraphs."

Consider this sentence: "It was a pretty day." There's nothing wrong with this sentence; it's grammatically correct. However, it lacks the specifics that make descriptions come alive. What exactly does pretty mean? Maybe the writer's idea of pretty is quite different from yours. And what time of day are we talking about here? What day of the week? If it's Saturday, you might see the day differently than if it is Tuesday. In short, after you read this sentence a picture might form in your mind that's not even close to what the writer intended. What's more, "It was a pretty day" is vacuous and boring.

If this telling sentence were changed to a showing paragraph, it might read like this: "The moment she opened her window that bright Saturday morning, she felt the freshness crackling in the air. The leaves on every tree sparkled with reflected sunlight. The rainbow of flowers lining the front walk shouted 'Spring!' And above it all, puffy white clouds scuttled across a brilliant blue sky."

Now you know exactly what the writer means by a pretty day. You can see the scene in your mind as

Using imagery, Show Not Tell transforms dry sentences into fascinating descriptions.

From "Telling Sentences"

It was a pretty day.

The rain fell on the roof.

Across the road the pastures were green.

Some girl had a yellow ribbon in her hair.

To "Showing Paragraphs"

The moment she opened her window that bright Saturday morning, she felt the freshness crackling in the air. The leaves on every tree sparkled with reflected sunlight. The rainbow of flowers lining the front walk shouted "Spring!" And above it all, puffy white clouds scuttled across a brilliant blue sky.

Late in the Spring evening, drops of cool rain began to fall on the windowpanes warmed by the sputtering fire in the cabin's hearth. Willow trees swayed in the slow breezes, whispering nightsongs to the tranquil waves on the pond. Straining to catch the moist drops of rain, brown leaves of grass filled themselves with water to store away for the new green shoots on warm afternoons of May.

clearly as if you were watching it in a movie.

When you use Show Not Tell, paragraphs form naturally and vividly. They seem to take on a life of their own. The effect is fun and easy to achieve. Just show the scene as if you were filming it.

Now, your turn. Do a cluster, then create a showing paragraph for each of the following telling sentences. (It's best to create a whole new scenario without using the original telling sentence.)

1. His desk was a mess.

2. The concert was enjoyable.

3. The meeting went well.

4. The man was driving too fast.

The best thing about Show Not Tell is that every writer will come up with his or her own unique description for each sentence. It's impossible to do it without letting your own personal style come through.

Writing instructor Diane Hamilton uses a game to demonstrate the Show Not Tell technique. First, she asks students to make a list of associations for a phrase like *dream house*. Then, using the words they've written down, each student draws a dream house. On a separate sheet, they write a description of that house. Hamilton then collects the descriptions, mixes them up, and passes them out again, so that each student has someone else's description. She then asks the students to draw the houses described, then hang the drawings on the wall. The original writer tries to find the new drawing of his or her dream house, then hangs the original drawing next to it. It's a fun, effective way to demonstrate the concept, and it also shows how much variation can occur between the writer's pen and reader's mind.

You can play similar games with your descriptions. Read them to other people and have them guess what the telling sentence is, or have them draw it, if it's an

A beginning writer "breaks the block."

June came from a family of writers. Both her parents had made money from writing — her mother as a novelist and her father as a college professor. Her older brother was a newspaperman and prided himself on his ability to write anywhere, anytime — on airplanes, in phone booths — regardless of how menacingly his deadline loomed.

All her life, June had been intimidated by this writing legacy and whenever she was faced with a situation that called for the written word, she begged off, claiming that the writing talent in her family was already taken.

As a junior executive in a marketing firm, she conducted a study of consumer trends that produced some breakthrough information. The editor of a trade magazine got wind of it and called June's boss, suggesting that June write an article about her findings. Seeing this as an opportunity for some positive exposure both for June and the firm, he promised the article would be written.

When she got the assignment, June was mortified. All her feelings of inadequacy bubbled to the surface. Every time she sat down to write, she got nothing for her efforts but sweaty palms and a wastebasket full of crumpled paper. The deadline got nearer every day, and still she hadn't written a word.

One day at lunch, June was lamenting her situation, when Pam, one of her coworkers, said, "I don't know what you're so uptight about. You're one of the best speakers I've ever heard. When you give a speech, it's organized, well written, and easy to understand. Why don't you just sit down and pretend you're giving a speech — only give it on paper?"

Without finishing her lunch, June rushed back to the office, sat down, and imagined herself on her feet, ready to address her favorite kind of audience. She breathed easily, her palms were dry, and the words flowed out as smoothly as if her mind were a laser printer. After weeks of writer's block, June wrote her story in one afternoon — and once the article was published, she had a reputation as one of the best writers in the office.

object. If they get it right, you've done a great job.

The Show Not Tell technique has many applications. You've seen how it can be used for characterization, action, and setting the scene. It's also effective for poetry and stories, and it's especially powerful in essays, compare/contrast tasks, and persuasive pieces.

Stages to a Complete Writing Process

Now that you know two ways to get started and a great technique for breathing life into your writing, you're ready to move on to a complete writing process. This process has been adapted from the California Writing Project and has been demonstrated to be effective for virtually any kind of writing you can name.

1. Prewriting

Clustering and fastwriting are both techniques for this stage of the writing process. At this point, you're simply building a foundation for the topic based on your knowledge, thoughts, and experiences.

2. Rough Draft

Here you begin to explore and expand on your ideas. Focus on content rather than on punctuation, grammar, or spelling. Remember to Show Not Tell as you write.

3. Sharing

This part of the process is very important. According to writing instructor Michael Carr, it is also the most overlooked. As writers, we are so close to our writing that it's difficult for us to judge objectively. In order to get some distance from your writing, you need to have someone else read it and give you feedback. Have a friend, colleague, spouse, or classmate read it and tell you which parts are really strong. Also have them point out any inconsistencies, unclear statements, or weak transitions. Here are some guidelines for sharing.

This writing process is effective for all forms of writing.

1. **Prewriting**   Clustering and fastwriting.

2. **Rough Draft**   Ideas are explored and expanded upon.

3. **Sharing**   A partner reads the draft and provides feedback.

4. **Revising**   From the feedback, revise work, and share again.

5. **Editing**   Correct all spelling, grammar, and punctuation.

6. **Rewriting**   Incorporate new content and editing changes.

7. **Evaluation**   Check to see the task is accomplished.

— Adapted from the California Writing Project

For the writer:

- Tell your reader what you were trying to accomplish by writing this piece.
- There is no right or wrong at this point, so leave your ego at the door. Welcome all feedback without emotional involvement. Later you can choose the input you wish to accept or disregard.
- Listen only. Don't try to clarify anything for the reader. If it's not there, it's not there!
- After the reader has given you feedback, it's okay to ask questions for the sake of clarification.

For the reader:

- Read for content only. Ignore grammar and spelling until later.
- First, tell the writer what words, phrases, and major parts work *best* for you as a reader.
- Tell him or her about any questions that came to mind as you read the piece.
- Tell the writer if you think this piece accomplishes the goals it set out to accomplish.
- Last, tell how it could be made even stronger and clearer.

4. Revising

Now that you have some feedback as to what's great and what needs work, go back and revise. Remember that you are the master of your writing, and you make the final decisions on which parts of the feedback to embrace and which to discard. Make use of the feedback you find helpful. Your goal is to write the best possible report, letter, or paper. After revising, share it with your partner again.

Many times the writing process will assume a loop or multiloop pattern.

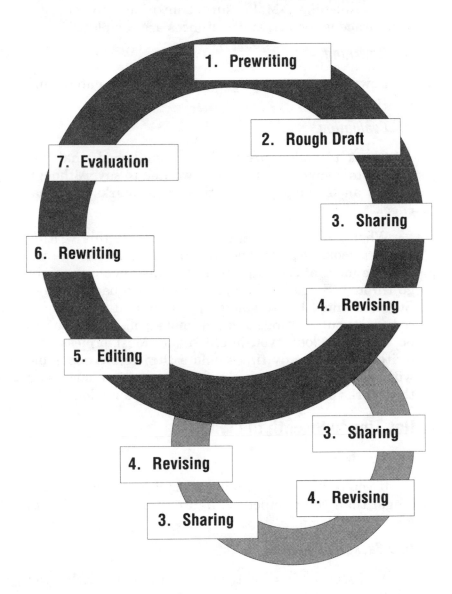

1. Prewriting

2. Rough Draft

7. Evaluation

3. Sharing

6. Rewriting

4. Revising

5. Editing

3. Sharing

4. Revising

4. Revising

3. Sharing

5. Editing

Finally, it's time to let the left-brain "editor" step in. At this stage, correct all spelling, grammar, and punctuation mistakes. Make sure transitions are smooth, verb usage is correct, and sentences are complete.

6. Rewriting

Rewrite your piece, incorporating new content and editing changes.

7. Evaluation

Check to make sure you've accomplished what you set out to do and said what you wanted to say. Although this is an ongoing process, this stage marks the final check.

When explained in the above manner, this writing process looks logical and linear. In practice, it can assume more of a loop pattern. For instance, you might go through Stages 1 through 4, then loop back through Stages 3 and 4 before going on to 5, 6, and 7. The more complex your writing, and the more polished it has to be, the more loops you might make. Most professional writers revise many times before they feel comfortable with what they've done. In fact, one writer once said that works of art are never finished, just abandoned.

Hot Tips to Smooth the Way

Start Early

If you're like most people, everything seems to take longer than you planned, so figure some extra time into your preparation.

Use Background Music

As discussed in Chapter 4, baroque music helps you relax and puts you into a resourceful state of mind.

 # Tips to Smooth the Way

- Start early.

- Use background music.

- Find the right time.

- Get some exercise.

- Read anything and everything.

- Layer the job.

- Use colors.

Find the Right Time

Some people do their best writing first thing in the morning; others wax poetic after everyone else has gone to bed. Find the right time for you.

Get Some Exercise

This keeps you fresh and provides good oxygen for the brain, both of which can help your state of mind while writing.

Read Anything and Everything

Magazines, newspapers, novels, nonfiction, cereal boxes, song lyrics, encyclopedias, books of quotes and proverbs, poems, comics, and children's literature — read 'em all. Reading keeps you in touch with life, language usage, and writing styles.

Layer the Job

It's easier to face a big writing project when it's broken down into smaller chunks. So resolve to work on one section at a time. Refer also to the Writing Process.

Use Colors

When writing your rough draft, use different colors for each section or idea. This helps you to see all of the parts of your paper better.

Hot Tips for Getting Unstuck

Here are some ways to get back on track when you run into writer's block.

Save Your Favorite Papers

Then, when you start getting too self-critical and it holds you back, read them. This reminds you that you really are a great writer, so you can move ahead with confidence.

 # Tips for Getting Unstuck

- Save your favorite papers.

- Put yourself on the other side.

- Get away from it.

- Break your routine.

- Change your writing tools.

- Change your environment.

- Talk to a child, or a group of children, about your project.

Put Yourself on the Other Side

Try to view whatever it is you're writing about from the opposite viewpoint for a while. This allows you to think about the problem objectively and creatively at the same time. Example: You're trying to sell someone something. Put yourself in the position of a person who's thinking, "I don't want this, I don't need it, I can't afford it." What would you have to say to get through to that person? What ideas or emotions would make them say, "Hey, I *do* need this"?

Get Away from It

Sometimes you have to physically set the writing aside and let your subconscious work on it. Go for a walk and then come back to it refreshed, or work on something else for a while.

Break Your Routine

Try writing at a different time of day, eating at a new ethnic restaurant, shopping at a different market, or taking a new route home from work. Doing things differently enables you to look at things in new ways and make connections you may not have seen before.

Change Your Writing Tools

If you usually use a word processor, try writing it by hand or typing.

Change Your Environment

Find a new place to do your writing. Park your car someplace with a view and write. Or just take your writing outside to the patio for a change.

Talk to Children About Your Project

Really, try it! Even if they don't completely understand the subject they usually have opinions and frequently can make you see your topic in a different light.

I Know I Know

☑ Check the box if you understand the concept:

☐ I know two ways to get started writing:

1 _____

2 _____

☐ I know how to Show Not Tell.

☐ I know all ideas are good ideas.

☐ I know writing is discovery.

☐ I know the stages to a complete writing process:

1 _____

2 _____

3 _____

4 _____

5 _____

6 _____

7 _____

☐ I know I have the "how-to's" and the confidence to write.

☐ I know I am a brilliant writer!

9

Work Your Own Memory Miracles!

Why should you read this chapter?

☑ Improve your capacity to remember facts, details, and "things to do."

☑ Easily memorize lists of names, numbers, and other items.

☑ Increase confidence for presentations and speeches.

☑ Remember names of people you've met.

Chances are, your life is so filled with appointments, budgets, work presentations, luncheon dates, people's birthdays, phone numbers, personal projects, and continuing education seminars that remembering specific details of anything seems an impossible task. That's why you need to learn the memory techniques in this chapter.

For many years, the doorman at the Canlis restaurant in Seattle amazed diners with his memory skills. As diners arrived, he would park their cars and never give them a ticket or write down a thing. There was a window near the front door, through which he could see diners as they prepared to leave. When they stepped out onto the sidewalk, their cars were there waiting for them. He always matched the right car to the right people.

Hundreds of people dined there every evening. How did he remember which face went with which car? We don't know what specific method he used, but we do know it is possible to devise your own methods of remembering things in an equally or even more impressive manner.

Dan Mikels, who has taught the memory class at SuperCamp, earned a television appearance on *That's Incredible,* by memorizing all the names, addresses, and phone numbers in the Los Angeles telephone directory. Ask him how he did it, and Mikels will modestly assure you that it wasn't really that incredible. Anyone can do it, he says, using his system of visual associations and a computer program to organize the numbers.

What would you say if I told you that your memory is just as phenomenal as that of the two people mentioned above? It's true! Experiments done on the human brain suggest that you may indeed remember every single bit of information you've ever been exposed to. This means you probably remember, right now, the names of all the children in your first-grade class. You also remember the address and phone number of every place

Dan Mikels, a past SuperCamp memory instructor, memorized the entire Los Angeles telephone directory by using visual associations.

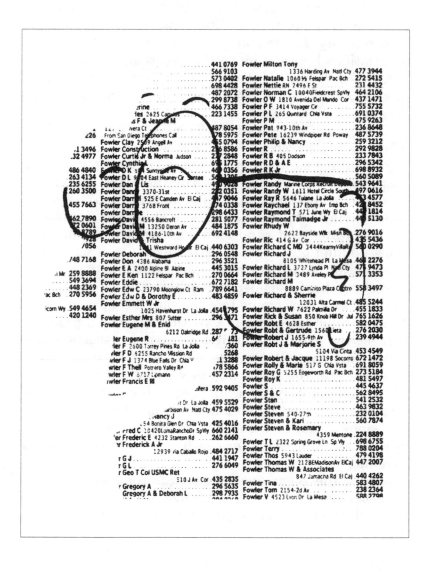

you've ever lived. You even remember how much you paid for lunch on the fifth day of your vacation in 1979.

Most of us have heard older people complain that their memories aren't what they used to be. Yet have you noticed that senior citizens seem to have almost total recall of events that happened many years ago — even though they can't remember what's taken place in the recent past? It might surprise you to learn that your capacity to remember facts and details can actually *increase* with age rather than diminish. That's because your memory is based on your ability to create links and associations between bits of information. The older you are, the more bits of information you have stored in your memory. Therefore, you have more possible links between the bits.

Here's a simple example. Think of a palm tree on a white sandy beach and the waves of an aquamarine lagoon rolling gently into the shore. Under the tree are a small table and two chairs. On the table stand two glasses of refreshing liquid. Now imagine you're a small child coming into that scene. As a child, you'd probably see the water and sand as a wonderful playground to splash in and build castles. After a session of hard play, you might be thirsty, and then you might see the refreshing drinks to quench your thirst.

Now imagine coming into the same scene as a young adult of nineteen or twenty. At this age, you'll probably still see the playful and thirst–quenching aspects of this delightful place. But you're also likely to inject some romance into the scene due to your exposure to travel advertising and your own personal experience. You might see yourself swimming languidly in the sea, casually sipping mai tai's under the palm tree with a dream lover or strolling along the beach with that person, hand in hand.

Enter the scene once again, this time as a middle-aged person. Perhaps you've fought in a war that was set in the tropics. Maybe you and your family went on a

Our memory is relative to age and life experiences.

As a child, both play and pleasure are likely to be the focus of rememberances.

As a young adult, romance and exotic locations become more significant.

As an adult, the mind recalls life's experiences: childish, romantic, and real.

vacation to a similarly idyllic island. Regardless, as you walk into the scene, your mind flashes through many associations including the childish, the romantic, and the real. As you age you're able to embellish the scene with more and more meaning, simply because you have more to draw upon than you did as a small child. The scene becomes more vivid due to the meaningful links you can make.

What does all this have to do with your memory? Simply put, the more you connect meaningful associations with a certain event, or theory, or set of facts, the more likely you are to have "collected" meaningful associations.

The Distinction Between Memory and Recall

When people say they don't have very good memories, they're actually talking about *recall*. They have difficulty recalling information that is already in their memories. Your memory stores everything and recalls only what it needs and what has meaning in your life.

Dan Mikels believes that many people seem to lose their ability to remember as they grow older because they stop "landmarking." Landmarks, says Mikels, are events in our lives that are new, interesting, and exciting and that serve as links to other bits of information in the memory chain.

Take for example your very first day on your first job. Chances are, you remember that day vividly. You may recall the people you met, where you had lunch, how the neighborhood looked, and what the weather was like. Although your chances of remembering the weather on any other random day are slim, you can remember it on that particular date because the day itself was a landmark, and it is *linked* to many other details and bits of information in your mind.

For most of us, our early lives are filled with many such landmarks. As we get older, the landmarks tend to

A distinction is made between memory and recall to understand how the brain stores and recalls information.

R
E
C
A
L
L

The mind stores everything and recalls only what it needs and what has meaning in life.

By living life fully, you create new memory links and increase your ability to remember facts, events, and new information.

With increased ability to recall details, an individual develops creativity and is more successful at problem-solving.

come farther and farther apart — partly because we tend to become set in our ways and do things the same way time after time, and partly because we have already done so much that most experiences are repeats of former experiences.

Your life doesn't have to be that way, however. To nudge your memory into high gear, Mikels suggests you do new things, eat new foods, go to new places. When you decide to dine out, go to a restaurant you've never been to before and order something you've never tasted. Take every opportunity to create new experiences — new landmarks. By living life to the fullest this way, you are creating new memory links and increasing your ability to remember all kinds of facts, events, and new information.

Forging new memory links also increases your personal creativity. As Peter Kline says in his book *The Everyday Genius* (Great Ocean Publishers, 1988), to be creative problem-solvers and constructive thinkers, "we must be able to draw freely and widely on the full range of our experience, which is the context of our memory." As you can imagine, a person with a large and varying bank of personal experiences — and *the skills to remember details* from experiences and plug them into new circumstances — will be vastly more creative than a person who has few life experiences.

Before you can learn to improve your recall ability, you need to know just what it is that makes things memorable.

What We Remember Best

Although your brain stores all the information you are exposed to during your life, you're most likely to recall information that is charged with meaning in one way or another. Generally, we remember best information that is characterized by one or more of the following:

You remember information best when it is characterized by these qualities:

■ Sensory associations, especially visual

■ Emotional context, such as love, happiness, and sorrow

■ Outstanding or different qualities

■ Intense associations

■ Necessities for survival

■ Personal importance

■ Repetition

■ First and last in a session

person tells you his or her phone number, you'll most likely remember it even if you don't write it down.

Repeated Items

I have a friend who was a C student in chemistry all the way through high school and college. Due to his career choice, he had to study the subject again as a graduate student. After his third or fourth course studying the same material, he remarked to me that it finally "sank in" just from repetition. (He got an A in the class that time!)

First and Last Items in a Session

When you're studying, or are in a class or meeting, you'll remember best the information you read or hear at the beginning and at the end of the session.

Now you're ready to learn some specific memory techniques and the key to using them effectively.

Association

The key to excellent recall is how we associate items in our memories. Some associations happen naturally, like in the scene with the sandy beach. Others may not be so obvious. You may even need to invent the association, which will take a conscious effort on your part. Since I use association in every one of the memory techniques that follow, you'll see many examples of this concept in action here.

You can use simple associations to remember isolated pieces of information, and more complex associations to remember difficult theories and bodies of information that contain many small, interrelated "chunks." For example, use this simple form of association to remember names and faces: When you meet someone, repeat the name out loud or to yourself. If you know others by the same name, picture this new person

Association techniques help you to remember names when you're introduced to new people.

with those people. Picture them all doing something active, like sitting around a table at a party laughing and talking, or skiing down a mountain together. Pick something you know one of them likes to do.

You can also pick a physical feature that stands out on the person you're meeting, like a prominent mole or large ears. Link this to their name — like Molly with a mole — or simply picture the letters of Molly's name written on those big ears. Having made the conscious effort to link the name of the person to something visual, your mind is likely to flash through the same visual association the next time you see Molly's face, producing her name as you smile and greet her.

The techniques described in the rest of this chapter rely heavily on the use of association, and as you do the suggested exercises, you'll become very adept at forming associations.

Linking

When you need to memorize a list of facts or terms that seem unrelated, you can link them together with a silly story that makes remembering easier. Suppose you have to remember the following lists of facts about several of the different tribes of American Indians:

Cheyenne
- lived in *tepees*
- killed *buffalo* for their skin and meat
- used *bow* and *arrow*

Nootka
- made houses out of *wood*
- caught *fish* for food with *harpoons*
- made *canoes* from *trees*

When using the linking technique, remember the following guidelines to make your associations memorable.

■ Use color and sensory *descriptions*.

■ *Act* them out.

■ Give them sexual *overtones*.

■ Make it *emotional*.

■ Be *outrageous*.

Creek
- built houses out of *straw* and *mud*
- hunted *deer*
- women made *clay pots* and *wove cloth*

Hopi
- women built houses out of *stone*
- ate mostly *corn*
- *kind, loving* people
- *men* wove *cloth*

Using the underlined key words, create silly stories to help you remember them. To recall the facts about the Cheyenne, think of this scene: "Shy Anne was so shy that she stayed in her *tepee* all day with her pet *buffalo* who wore a big yellow *bow* in his hair and painted red *arrows* all over the walls of the tepee."

To remember the facts about the Creek Indians, think of this story: "I went down to the *creek*, waded through lots of thick, sticky *mud*, through wet, prickly *straw* that tickled my legs, and I saw these *deer* swimming down the creek with *clay pots* on their heads and rolls of colorful *woven cloth* sticking out of the pots." It would be pretty hard to forget a ridiculous scene like that, wouldn't it?

Now make up your own stories about the Nootka and Hopi Indians. Use lots of color and sensory descriptions; act them out; give them sexual overtones; make it emotional. Be outrageous! The more outrageous, the more likely you are to remember.

In our programs, we show students how they can use linking to learn the names of a chain of countries that border on one another. For instance, if you had an airplane with fuel to take you five thousand miles and you flew southeast from Italy, you would pass over Greece, Turkey, Iraq, Iran, Pakistan, and India before you finally splashed down in the Indian Ocean. You can

Linking techniques help when memorizing a list of geographical terms or patterns.

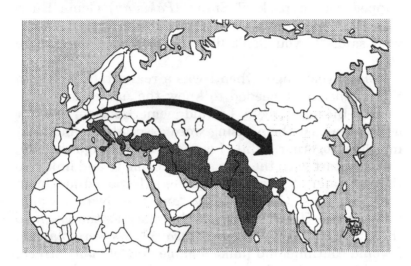

If you had an airplane with fuel to take you five thousand miles and you flew southeast from Italy, you would pass over Greece, Turkey, Iraq, Iran, Pakistan, and India before you finally splashed down in the Indian Ocean. Here's how to link them:

I was sitting in a restaurant eating spaghetti (*Italy*), and I yelled to a woman passing by, "Hey, don't eat here, it's greasy!" (*Greece*). Then the chef, who was really a turkey (*Turkey*), heard and started chasing me, threatening to kill me with an oven rack (*Iraq*). I ran and I ran (*Iran*) and tripped over a pack of Stan's (*Pakistan*) Genie Dust. When I opened the package, out blew an Indian (*India*) who said, "If you don't like the food, eat somewhere else!"

remember those countries like this: I was sitting in a restaurant eating spaghetti (*Italy*), and I yelled to a woman passing by, "Hey, don't eat here, it's greasy" (*Greece*). Then the chef, who was really a turkey (*Turkey*), heard and started chasing me, threatening to kill me with an oven rack (*Iraq*). I ran and I ran (*Iran*) and tripped over a pack of Stan's (*Pakistan*) Genie Dust. When I opened the package, out blew an Indian (*India*) who said, "If you don't like the food, eat somewhere else."

Many years ago, when I was a real estate broker in San Francisco, I needed to know the names and locations of the city streets. I would memorize them in order as I drove past them, using word associations and linking them together. While I was driving through the city, I would start with the first street I came to and link it to the next and so on. For example, if I started at Union and drove past Green, Vallejo, and Broadway, I would imagine the *Union* army marching across the *green* to the city of *Vallejo,* where *Broadway* shows were playing. I would continue and make a game of how many streets I could remember from one end of the city to the other, starting at the beginning in my mind and repeating often. It was great memory practice, plus it was a benefit to me to know every street.

The Peg System

The peg system can be used to memorize any list of items. A list of numbers that are matched up with rhyming words or visual cues is used as a constant (your pegboard), which becomes firmly planted in your memory, and the list of items you need to memorize is plugged into your peg list.

Here is the list Dan Mikels uses:

1. Sun
2. Eyes
3. Triangle

A peg system matches numbers with rhyming words or visual cues. Make up your own list of words.

Number	Rhyming Word or Visual Cue
1	_____
2	_____
3	_____
4	_____
5	_____
6	_____
7	_____
8	_____
9	_____
10	_____
11	_____
12	_____
13	_____
14	_____
15	_____
16	_____
17	_____
18	_____
19	_____
20	_____

4. Four-square
5. Fingers
6. Sticks
7. 7-Up
8. Octopus
9. Baseball
10. Hen
11. Fence
12. Eggs
13. Cat
14. Money
15. Boxing
16. Car
17. Magazine
18. Vote
19. TV
20. Phone

Note that each of the words has a visual aspect, and a logical connection can be made between each number and its matching word. Some connections are obvious and some take a little thinking. Numbers 1 through 8 are easy, right? Just to make sure you get the rest, I'll point out the connections:

9. There are *9* players on a baseball team.
10. *10* rhymes with hen.
11. See two planks of a fence as the number *11*.
12. A *dozen* eggs.
13. *13* is "unlucky," just like a black cat.
14. As in the expression, *"One (1) for (4) the money, two for the show, three to get ready, four to go."*
15. *15* rounds in a boxing match.
16. You must be *16* to drive a car.
17. *Seventeen* magazine.
18. You must be *18* to vote.
19. *19* inches is a standard television size.
20. It often costs *20* cents to make a phone call.

Each of the words Dan Mikels uses in his peg list contain visual aspects and logical connections between each number and its matching word.

1.	*Sun*	
2.	*Eyes*	
3.	*Triangle*	
4.	*Four-Square*	
5.	*Fingers*	
6.	*Sticks*	
7.	*7-Up*	
8.	*Octopus*	
9.	*Baseball*	9 players on a baseball team.
10.	*Hen*	10 rhymes with hen.
11.	*Fence*	See two planks of a fence as the number 11.
12.	*Eggs*	A dozen eggs.
13.	*Cat*	13 is "unlucky," just like a black cat.
14.	*Money*	As in the expression, "One (1) for (4) the money, two for the show, three to get ready, four to go."
15.	*Boxing*	15 rounds in a boxing match.
16.	*Car*	You must be 16 to drive a car.
17.	*Magazine*	*Seventeen* magazine.
18.	*Vote*	You must be 18 to vote.
19.	*TV*	19 inches is a standard television size.
20.	*Phone*	It often costs 20 cents to make a phone call.

Take a few moments to become familiar with the list. Then look at this new list of the first twenty U.S. presidents. Memorize their names by plugging each name into the first list — like matching 1–sun to 1–George Washington and 2–eyes to 2–John Adams.

1. George Washington
2. John Adams
3. Thomas Jefferson
4. James Madison
5. James Monroe
6. John Quincy Adams
7. Andrew Jackson
8. Martin Van Buren
9. William Henry Harrison
10. John Tyler
11. James K. Polk
12. Zachary Taylor
13. Millard Fillmore
14. Franklin Pierce
15. James Buchanan
16. Abraham Lincoln
17. Andrew Johnson
18. Ulysses S. Grant
19. Rutherford B. Hayes
20. James Garfield

The key to plugging new words or terms into the peg system is to make them as visual as possible. Involve your senses. Make the associations colorful, exaggerated, imaginative, and absurd. Refer back to the section in this chapter on "What We Remember Best" for ideas.

Now let's try plugging in. I'll help you get started with the first ten items, and you can find your own associations for the rest of the list.

1. Sun, George Washington — Imagine *George washing one* pane of his window so the sun can

Use your peg system and visual associations to memorize lists of individuals or items.

1.	*Sun*	George Washington
2.	*Eyes*	John Adams
3.	*Triangle*	Thomas Jefferson
4.	*Four-Square*	James Madison
5.	*Fingers*	James Monroe
6.	*Sticks*	John Quincy Adams
7.	*7-Up*	Andrew Jackson
8.	*Octopus*	Martin Van Buren
9.	*Baseball*	William Henry Harrison
10.	*Hen*	John Tyler
11.	*Fence*	James K. Polk
12.	*Eggs*	Zachary Taylor
13.	*Cat*	Millard Fillmore
14.	*Money*	Franklin Pierce
15.	*Boxing*	James Buchanan
16.	*Car*	Abraham Lincoln
17.	*Magazine*	Andrew Johnson
18.	*Vote*	Ulysses S. Grant
19.	*TV*	Rutherford B. Hayes
20.	*Phone*	James Garfield

shine in. Act it out yourself, moving your whole arm and hand around and around in the shape of the sun.

2. Eyes, John Adams — See two eyes, look closer and closer until you see nothing but *atoms* spinning, and from the nucleus of one atom comes, mysteriously, the word *John.*

3. Triangle, Thomas Jefferson — Imagine that *Thomas* and *Jeff*, his *son*, are in love with the same woman; it's a nasty love triangle.

4. Four-square, James Madison — *James* is *mad at his son* because they're playing four-square and the son is winning.

5. Fingers, James Monroe — Imagine *James* holding hands with Marilyn *Monroe.*

6. Sticks, John Quincy Adams — John Quincy's *Adam's* apple is bobbing up and down, up and down, and you are trying to hit it with a *cue* stick.

7. 7-Up, Andrew Jackson — See Michael *Jackson* doing a 7-Up commercial.

8. Octopus, Martin Van Buren — *Martin's van* is *burning* and an octopus comes along to put out the fire, holding one hose in each of his eight tentacles.

9. Baseball, William Harrison — *William's hairy son* is throwing a baseball. See the number "9" on his uniform, and see his hairy arms throw the ball.

10. Hen, John Tyler — *John* the *tiler* has ten hens and each one is balancing a tile on its beak.

Get the idea? These are my silly associations, but you could have come up with your own. Try it now with the second half of the list — and remember, the more outrageous the better. Then get a blank piece of paper, close the book, and write down the first twenty U.S. presidents, using the peg system. I'll bet you can

Peg systems work best when associations are colorful, exaggerated, imaginative, and absurd.

1 *Sun*

George Washington

Imagine *George washing one* pane of his window so the sun can shine in.

Act it out yourself, moving your whole arm and hand around and around in the shape of the sun.

2 *Eyes*

John Adams

See two eyes, look closer and closer until you see nothing but *atoms* spinning, and from the nucleus of one atom comes, mysteriously, the word *John.*

3 *Triangle*

Thomas Jefferson

Imagine that *Thomas* and *Jeff,* his *son,* are in love with the same woman; it's a nasty love triangle!

remember most of them on your first try!

You can also create your own peg list using numbers and words that are more familiar or that make more sense to you. For example, you might want to use numbers and words that rhyme. Here is a peg list of rhyming words: 1–sun, 2–glue, 3–knee, 4–door, 5–hive, 6–sticks, 7–heaven, 8–gate, 9–vine, 10–hen.

Once you are comfortable with your list, you can use and reuse it to memorize any list of items. If the list is longer than twenty items, you can either extend your peg list or repeat it. If your peg list has twenty items and you must remember a list of forty items, number 21 will be linked to number 1, number 25 will be linked to 5, number 30 to 10, and so on. Using the presidents as an example: The twenty-first president was Chester A. Arthur. Link him to number one, George Washington. Imagine George washing one pane of his window so the sun can shine in. As you act it out, moving your arm around in a circle like the shape of the sun, the window becomes cleaner and cleaner, and it's easier and easier to see outside. What do you see outside? Why, it's Chester, a dog with a weird bark, saying "Arth! Arth! Arth!"

The Location Method

To use the location method, pick a place that is familiar to you, such as your home or car, and locate whatever you'd like to remember there.

Suppose you want to remember a grocery list of tomatoes, noodles, bread, bananas, and spaghetti sauce. You know you'll be driving home from work in your car and need to stop at the supermarket on the way. Take a moment and imagine this. The tomatoes are smashed into the glove compartment. You shut the compartment door, and they ooze out. The noodles are hanging over the rearview mirror, the bread pops out of the cassette player as toast, the bananas are squished on the floor, and the spaghetti sauce jar is balancing on your head, bubbling over and running down your face.

Peg systems can be extended or repeated to continue memorizing long lists of items.

21 *Sun*

Chester A. Arthur

Link him to number one, George Washington.

Imagine George washing one pane of his window so the sun can shine in.

As you act it out, moving your arm around in a circle like the shape of the sun, the window becomes cleaner and cleaner, and it's easier and easier to see outside.

What do you see outside? Why, it's Chester the dog, saying "Arth! Arth! Arth!"

Now when you get in your car after work and want to remember what to buy, you have only to look at the glove compartment and the whole series of images starts flooding back to you.

The more *unusual* and *ridiculous* the image, the easier it is to remember. Suppose you need to remember to call your best friend and wish her a happy birthday. Close your eyes and picture your best friend sitting at an old, bizarre-looking table, wearing a clown suit (or maybe not wearing anything) and balancing a birthday candle on her nose. On the table a red-hot phone is ringing. Your friend picks up the phone, and it's you calling. Now take that picture and mentally place it as a movie that is playing on your front door. Tonight, when you go home, stop at your door and see what's playing. You'll remember that you wanted to call your best friend.

Scott Bornstein, an authority on memory who taught at the first SuperCamp and many since, has a peg system that can be used in conjunction with the location method. His peg list fits in a classroom: 1–blackboard, 2–light switch, 3–floor, 4–ceiling, 5–book, 6–phone, 7–door, 8–window, 9–chair, and so on.

I also use the location method in connection with the peg method, but my peg words are connected to locations in my home. When I want to remember something, I simply walk through my home in my mind. You can create your own location system, filling in the following list by walking through your own home and picking several distinctive features from each room. My house:

Entry Way
1.
2.
3.
Living Room
4.
5.
6.

The Location Method involves using a familiar place and exaggerated images.

Dining Room
7.
8.
9.
Kitchen
10.
11.
12.
Bedroom
13.
14.
15.
Bathroom
16.
17.
18.

Most of us (especially kinesthetic learners) can walk around our homes in the dark, knowing instinctively where things are without actually seeing them. Try this sometime: Get up out of bed when it's still dark and walk into the next room. Reach for the light switch and turn on the light. You probably won't bump into anything as you move about and will make contact with the light switch on your first or second try, even if you can't see it. Your body knows its way around your home, so it should be no problem to close your eyes and imagine each room. Memorizing a location list like this for your peg system is a natural.

I always use this method when giving a presentation. I first make a Mind Map (see Chapter 7) of the main points, with branches for subtopics. I number the points in the order they will be presented; then I make an association with each item on the peg system. (1) My introduction for what I will be talking about is associated with (and written on) the front door, (2) the light switch is discussing (shedding light on) who I am and why I am qualified to talk about this topic . . . and so on.

It takes only a short time to make these associa-

The location method can be used with the peg method, connecting words to locations.

begin here

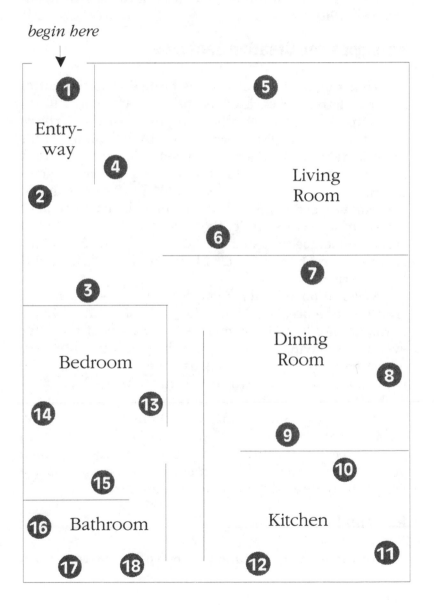

tions, and it is time well spent. It saves me time in preparing my presentation, and I can relax and give my talk confidently without worrying that I'll forget what I wanted to say.

Once again, refer back to our list of "What We Remember Best" to infuse your associations with memorable qualities.

Acronyms and Creative Sentences

An acronym is a word that is formed from the initial letter or letters or each of the parts of a group of items or compound terms. Mothers Against Drunk Drivers uses the very effective acronym MADD. Many other organizations and citizen's groups also have names that are acronyms. We are all familiar with many other acronyms, such as NATO, OPEC, and NASA. As individuals, we can use acronyms creatively to help us remember information. For example, the names of the Great Lakes can be remembered using the acronym HOMES — *H* for Huron, *O* for Ontario, *M* for Michigan, *E* for Erie, and *S* for Superior.

A variation on this memory method is the use of creative sentences. An elementary school teacher I know helps her students to memorize the planets of the solar system by having them recite this sentence: "My very educated mother just served us nine pizzas." Take the first letter from each word, you have M–V–E–M–J–S–U–N–P. From this, it's easy to remember the planets in order from the Sun — Mercury, Venus, Earth, Mars, Jupiter, Saturn, Uranus, Neptune, and Pluto. Make up your own creative sentences and acronyms the next time you need to remember a number of items; then dazzle your colleagues with your phenomenal memory.

Hot Tips!

All the memory techniques you've just learned work

Acronyms and creative sentences are used to memorize a sequence of names.

An *acronym* is a word formed from the initial letters of a group of items.

Huron

Ontario

Michigan

Erie

Superior

Creative sentences also use the first letter of each word.

My	Mercury
Very	Venus
Educated	Earth
Mother	Mars
Just	Jupiter
Served	Saturn
Us	Uranus
Nine	Neptune
Pizzas	Pluto

very well when used alone and even more effectively if used in combination with one another. You saw how the location method could be used in combination with a peg system, for instance, and how to build on a peg system by linking items in one list to items in successive lists.

Now, here are some tips for keeping your memory in tip-top working order and making the most effective use of any memory technique.

Remember to Remember

Make a conscious effort. We need to stop and take a moment to make an association, to remember to use our techniques. How often have you met someone and as soon as you walk away, you can't remember his or her name? That's because you forgot to remember at the moment you were hearing it! Next time, take the time to make an association that will flash back as soon as you see that person again.

Practice Using Your Memory

Use every opportunity to hone your memory skills by using them often, even for things that aren't essential to remember. As you drive to your destination, for instance, try to remember the names of all the streets or freeway exits by linking them together in a silly story.

Make Your Associations Specific and Clear, Rather Than General

Instead of seeing words, see images that involve distinct action, color, and noise. That way, each association will stand on its own.

Remember Something Else

If you have problems recalling the exact piece of information you need, consciously create a link by remembering something else that's related to it. For

Tips for Memory Techniques

▓ Remember to remember.

▓ Practice using your memory.

▓ Make your associations specific and clear, rather than general.

▓ Remember something else.

▓ Mind Map your lessons and presentations.

▓ Imbue it with meaning.

▓ Review your material.

▓ Take many breaks while studying or reviewing something lengthy.

▓ Be healthy.

example, if you can't remember the sixth president, think of the fifth or the seventh. Many times this will bring back the information you're searching for.

Mind Map Your Lessons and Presentations

Mind Mapping is a natural memory tool because it uses color and symbols to create visual images, and as we've seen, visual associations are extremely vivid. Plus, mapping makes it possible to make visual links between bits of information.

Imbue It with Meaning

Ask yourself, "What's in it for me?" Find a personal reason for remembering, and reward yourself when you're successful.

Review Your Material

This is very important. Studies show that you will remember the information a little bit longer each time you review. When you are trying to learn something new, review it immediately, then again after twenty-four hours, then after a week, after two weeks, a month, and six months. Thereafter, you should be able to remember it if you review it once every six months. When reviewing, say it out loud. This adds a sensory association to it that you'll find easier to recall.

Take Many Breaks While Studying or Reviewing Something Lengthy

Since you remember best the information you hear or see first and last in a learning session, it follows that if you take many breaks, you will remember more of the information in the middle. Try to keep your sessions between twenty and forty minutes long, with breaks to move around, eat a snack, or get a drink of water. Take a mini–stretch break even more often.

Success using these memory skills occurs at all ages and in many different settings.

Grant DePorter, the author's son, grew up watching *The Brady Bunch* on television and knows the kids' names by heart, from youngest to oldest. He uses this television family for his linking method. When he had to remember a short list of events or facts for a test at school, he would link them in order to the Brady kids. He would then create an association to each and match something specific or ridiculous to each personality, remembering silly episodes and adventures from the television series.

Grant is a graduate of the first SuperCamp, which was held in the summer of 1982. He used the memory techniques he learned at SuperCamp to study for the SAT (Scholastic Aptitude Test). He had taken the test previously and scored a 66 percent on the vocabulary section. Before taking it a second time, he skipped two days of school and memorized an entire vocabulary book of more than 2,000 words — and raised his score to 99 percent! Every six months since then, he has reviewed the book. Now, years later, he still knows those words.

He continued to use his memory skills through college and graduate school, and now he uses them at work. As a new managing director of a restaurant, he memorized 165 employee names, first and last, his first day on the job.

Be Healthy

Naturally, your memory works best when you are in good physical condition. So get enough rest, eat properly, exercise, and breathe fresh air every day. A healthy body makes a happy mind.

I Know I Know

☑ Check the box if you understand the concept:

❑ I know eight characteristics that make things memorable:

1 _____   5 _____
2 _____   6 _____
3 _____   7 _____
4 _____   8 _____

❑ I know how to use these methods for remembering lists, names, faces, facts, and theories:

❑ Association   ❑ Linking

❑ Peg System   ❑ Location Method

❑ Acronyms   ❑ Creative Sentences

❑ I know I must "remember to remember."

❑ I know my memory is incredible.

Blast Off with Power Reading

Why should you read this chapter?

Dramatically improve your reading speed.

Improve comprehension and memory.

Increase vocabulary and develop your data bank.

Spend less time reading so you can do other things.

For many people, reading is a chore. Have you ever reached the bottom of a page and asked yourself, "What did I just read?" How often do you find yourself backing up to reread something, sometimes for the third or fourth time? Or do you ever find yourself stuck on one word because you're in a trancelike state?

These days, most people have to read a tremendous volume of material just to keep from getting buried in paper — at home, at the office, at school. Even if you subscribe to one newspaper and nothing else, you probably have more than you can read each day. Think about all the other reading material that's part of your life as well: magazines, how-to and self-help books, professional publications, memos, junk mail, novels, proposals, textbooks, and newsletters. If you actually read all this information word by word, you'd wind up spending all your time reading, with no time for anything else. If you're like most people, though, you either let your reading pile up until it reaches Himalayan proportions — then toss it — or you've devised methods of going through it without actually reading every word.

Very few people, for example, read the whole newspaper every day. (But after you learn the techniques in this chapter, you could if you wanted to. And think how well informed you would be if you did!) Rather than read the whole thing, you're more likely to read the stories that catch your immediate attention, then scan the rest of the paper for headlines, subheads, photos, photo captions, ads, "teasers," and anything else that stands out.

As you go through the paper in this way, your mind is comprehending, sorting, and storing all kinds of information. It's a method of reading that can be adapted for other types of material, and I'll show you how. This chapter will teach you how to experience reading, not as a chore to be put off as long as possible but as an enjoyable and satisfying skill. Like most of the learning skills in this book, the most important thing you can do to make these reading techniques work for you is to use

Everyday reading is likely to consist of scanning for attention-grabbing print, comprehending, sorting, and storing the information.

Banner-Tribune

SuperCamp students discover fun and excitement while learning how to learn!

Power Reading Blasts Off!

At SuperCamp, students learn new skills in accelerated learning that they take home with them to improve their schoolwork. One of their favorite SuperCamp classes is "Power Reading" where they learn speed reading methods to boost speed and comprehension. Throughout the day students are rewarded with constantly seeing their progress, and exploring new skills in reading.

With their new skills in reading techniques students discover they have the potential to boost comprehension and memory recall, along with speed.

Instructors teach students leading edge reading techniques which help students further discover the joy of reading, which in turn provides more time for fun.

> *Power Reading is fun and easy to learn!*

SuperCamp Students Go For It!

Between the fun of learning how to learn and the excitement of discovering the valuable resources inside themselves, students at SuperCamp learn new forms of challenging themselves.

One technique to reaching beyond personal limitations is the skill of "Going For It!" Used to improve self-confidence and motivation, students learn of their inner resources and capabilities to perform to the best of their abilities.

Applied to academic areas, "Going For It!" provides incentive to improve grades and reach for the rewards of improved learning. Used in areas of communication and relationship building, it allows students to discover the joy of reaching beyond their comfort zones.

them! The more you practice, the faster you'll be able to read — and we almost always like doing those things at which we excel.

Now let's get started! Since most of us feel more accomplished when we can see how far we've progressed, we'll start with a test that measures how quickly (or slowly) you read now.

Using an egg timer or a watch with a second hand, read the following selection for one minute. When your time is up, note where you left off. Start now.

The Nature of Water: Commonplace But Unique

Water is the most common substance on the face of the Earth. Surface water occupies more than 70 percent of the area of our planet, and it occurs to greater or lesser degree in the ground, air, and organisms everywhere.   5

Apparently the amount of moisture in existence is finite and remains constant through time — past, present, and future. There is now as much water as there ever was, or ever will be. It changes from one form to another, and moves from one place to another, but it   10
is neither created nor destroyed. Theoretically, it is possible that some of the water of your morning shower is the same that was used to wash Jesus' feet two thousand years ago, or was drunk by a brontosaurus fifty million years in the past.   15

Water is a remarkable substance and absolutely unique in several important characteristics. For example, it is the only known substance that is found naturally in all three states in which matter can occur: liquid, solid, gaseous. The great majority of the Earth's moisture is in the form of water. Water can be changed   20
to the gaseous form (water vapor) by *evaporation* or to the solid form (ice) by *freezing*. Water vapor can be converted to water by *condensation* or directly to ice by *sublimation*. Ice is convertible to water by *melting* or to

water vapor by *sublimation*. In each of these processes 25
there is either a gain or a loss of heat. Moisture in
plants can be passed through leaves into the air as
vapor by a process called *transpiration*.

Life is impossible without water; every living thing
depends on water for continuance of its life processes. 30
Watery solutions in organisms dissolve or disperse
nutrients for nourishment. Chemical reactions that can
take place only in a solution create energy from the
nutrients. Most waste products are carried away in
solutions. Indeed, the total mass of every living thing is 35
more than half water, the proportion ranging from
about 60 percent for some animals to more than 95
percent for some plants.

Water is a substance that has many unusual
properties. One of the most striking is its liquidity at 40
ordinary temperatures. It remains in a liquid state at
temperatures found at most places on the Earth's
surface. No other common substance is liquid at
ordinary Earth temperatures. The liquidity of water is
thus a normal state and greatly enhances its versatility 45
as an active agent in the atmosphere, lithosphere, and
biosphere.

Another environmentally important characteristic of
water is its great heat capacity. When something is
warmed, it absorbs energy and its temperature rises as 50
a result. When water is warmed, however, it can absorb
an enormous amount of energy without showing it by a
rise in temperature. Water's heat capacity is exceeded
by no other common substance except ammonia. The
practical result is that bodies of water are very slow to 55
warm up during the daytime or in summer, and
conversely, are very slow to cool off during the night or
in winter. Thus water bodies have a moderating effect
on surrounding temperatures by serving as reservoirs of
warmth during winter and having a cooling influence in 60
summer.

Most substances contract as they grow colder, but

when water freezes into ice, it expands. This quality makes ice less dense than water, and it allows ice to float on and near the surface of water, as icebergs and ice floes do. If ice were denser than water, it would sink to the bottom of lakes and oceans, where melting would be virtually impossible, and eventually many water bodies would become ice-choked. 65

Water normally responds to the pull of gravity and moves downward, but it is also capable of moving upward against the attraction of gravity under certain circumstances. This is because water has extremely high surface tension, which means that it can stick to itself and pull itself together. The water molecules stick closely together, and they wet the surfaces with which they come in contact. The high surface tension and wetting ability combine to allow water to climb upward. This climbing capability is most notable in situations where water is confined in small pore spaces or narrow tubes. In such restricted confinement, water can sometimes climb upward for many inches or even feet, in an action called *capillarity*. Capillarity enables water to circulate upward through rock and soil, or through roots and stems of plants. 70 75 80 85

Of all its interesting attributes, however, perhaps the most significant capability of water as an active agent in the landscape is its ability to dissolve other substances. Water can dissolve almost any substance, and it is sometimes referred to as the "universal solvent." It functions in effect as a mild acid, dissolving some things quickly and in large quantities; others slowly and in minute proportions. As a result, water in nature is nearly always impure; i.e., it contains various other chemicals in addition to its hydrogen and oxygen atoms. 90 95

Push your reading skills to catch up with your mental ability by letting go of myths you hold about reading.

Reading is hard.

You shouldn't use your finger to read.

Reading must be done one word at a time.

You must read slowly to comprehend the material.

Now, count the number of lines you read and multiply by nine. This is your reading speed for the first test.

Exploding the Myths

Remember how you learned to read, way back in elementary school? First you learned the letters; then you began to put them together to form words. You read one word at a time back then. By second grade or so, you could comprehend whole phrases without thinking of the individual words. But some of us never progressed beyond this level. Now it's time to push your reading skills to catch up with your mental abilities, and the first step is to put aside some of the myths you hold about reading.

- Reading is hard.
- You shouldn't use your finger to read.
- Reading must be done one word at a time.
- You must read slowly to comprehend the material.

If you hold any of these beliefs, get rid of them right now! Replace them with the explanations below, and you'll already be on your way to becoming a better reader.

Reading Is Easy

Though learning how to read is a very *complex* process, it is one which the human brain is certainly capable of handling. Most of us learned how to read by the age of six or seven, and with the increased mental ability of adulthood, we are capable of even greater feats.

It's Okay to Read with Your Finger

Even though you may have been taught not to read with your finger (possibly because you used it to point at one word at a time, which slowed you down), you *can*

Replacing old myths with new ideas is the first step in developing new reading skills.

- Reading is easy.

- It's okay to read with your finger.

- You can read many words at a time.

- You can read fast and still comprehend.

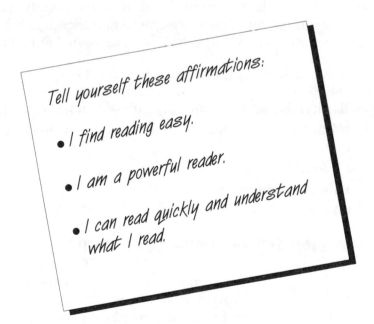

Tell yourself these affirmations:

- I find reading easy.

- I am a powerful reader.

- I can read quickly and understand what I read.

and *should* take up the habit again now! The difference is that you will now use your finger to guide your eyes *rapidly* through your reading material. The trick is always to move it a little bit faster than you think you can read.

You Can Read More than One Word at a Time

Actually, reading one word at a time decreases comprehension because the individual words are not viewed in context with others, and your mind must work harder to get the whole idea.

You Can Read Fast and Still Comprehend

Reading slowly can be pure drudgery for a brain as highly developed and quick to react as that of a human being. Chances are, you read slowly because you think you must in order to comprehend more completely. But the truth is, if you have problems comprehending what you're reading, it may be *because* you read too slowly. (The exception, of course, is when reading extremely complex subjects such as physics or microbiology.)

So instead of holding yourself back with negative thoughts that clog your brain and drag you down, tell yourself:

- I find reading easy.
- I am a powerful reader.
- I can read quickly and understand what I read.

Instant Hot Tips — "Getting into State"

Your physical and mental states are important keys to being an excellent reader. Take a few moments before each reading session to adjust your physical and mental position. This is called "getting into state," and it can double your reading speed instantly. Try this simple routine before beginning.

Tips to Reading

- "Get into state."

- Minimize distractions.

- Sit up straight and on the front of the chair.

- Take a moment to calm your mind.

- Use your finger or other pointer.

- Preview your material.

Minimize Distractions

Start by finding a calm, peaceful place to read. As we discussed in "Setting the Stage" (Chapter 4), music can be helpful. Try listening to baroque music timed at sixty beats per minute. This music is known to put people into a relaxed yet alert state because it simulates the average resting heart rate. It also keeps your freewheeling, artistic right brain busy, while allowing your logical left brain to focus on the task at hand.

Sit Up Straight and on the Front Edge of Your Chair

It's a fact that many high-powered corporate presidents wear out the front edges of their chairs first. Place your feet flat on the floor and prop your book on a table or desk in front of you.

Take a Moment to Calm Your Mind

Close your eyes, take a deep breath, and let yourself relax as you imagine a very peaceful place — perhaps a place you've been to before. Focus all of your concentration on this place. Keeping your eyes closed, allow your eyes to drift upward behind your closed lids for a few moments as you see, hear, and feel this place of peace. When you open your eyes, be aware of how relaxed you feel. Look up, then move your eyes to your book and begin reading.

Use Your Finger or Other Pointer

Because your eyes naturally follow a moving object, it is helpful for them to have a guide to follow as they move down the page. Try this exercise: Go back to the beginning of the chapter and use your finger to underline each line as you read it. Push your eyes quickly through the material by moving your finger a little bit faster than you think you can read. Resist stopping or backing up.

Your eyes naturally follow movement. Use your finger to push your eyes line by line down the page.

Preview Your Material

Before reading, browse through the material as though you were window-shopping before a spending spree. Scan the table of contents, the chapter headings, any boldface and italicized print, graphics and their captions, chapter summaries, the author's biography, and anything else that stands out. With a little preparation, you will know what to expect and your mind will already have a good idea of the ideas to be presented. To see how useful it can be to preview, try this little test:

Read the following paragraph, then summarize its contents.

> The icy ghost appeared to him from out of the dark as he surveyed from his position atop the graceful lady of steel. "Yet eyes deceive," Captain Smith thought, and failed to stop her momentum. Moments later the festive celebration of 2,000 was smashed to bits. *Carpathia,* 58 miles away, caught the SOS and raced to the rescue of a fortunate 705, one of whom remarked, years later, "She turned her deck away from us as though to hide from our sight the awful spectacle."

Did you have some difficulty understanding what this paragraph is about? If you had known by previewing that this is a description of the night in 1912 when the passenger liner *Titanic* struck an iceberg and sank, perhaps it would have been easier to understand. Read it again in this context.

Now, using the tips I've just given you, read the following article about gorillas and see how much you've improved! Be sure to check your physiology: Sit up straight on the edge of your seat, feet flat on the floor, book propped in front of you. Take a moment to calm your mind and focus your concentration. Set your timer for one minute, look up for a moment, then down at the page and begin. Remember to use your finger!

Previewing reading material increases comprehension and improves recall.

The icy ghost appeared to him from out of the dark as he surveyed from his position atop the graceful lady of steel. "Yet eyes deceive," Captain Smith thought and failed to stop her momentum. Moments later the festive celebration of 2,000 was smashed to bits. *Carpathia,* 58 miles away, caught the SOS and raced to the rescue of a fortunate 705, one of whom remarked, years later, "She turned her deck away from us as though to hide from our sight the awful spectacle."

Making Friends with Mountain Gorillas
by Dian Fossey

For the past three years I have spent most of my days with wild mountain gorillas. Their home, and mine, has been the misty wooded slopes of the Virunga range, eight lofty volcanos — the highest is 14,787 feet — shared by three African nations, Rwanda, Uganda, 5 and the Democratic Republic of the Congo.

During this time I have become well acquainted with many of the gorillas, and they with me. They roam the mountain slopes and saddles in groups, and several groups now accept my presence almost as a member. I 10 can approach to within a few feet of them, and some, especially the juveniles and young adults, have come even closer, picked up my camera strap, and examined the buckle on my knapsack. One has even played with the laces on my boots, though I have a feeling that he 15 did not suspect that the boots were, in fact, connected with me.

I know the gorillas as individuals, each with his own traits and personality, and, mainly for identification in my hundreds of pages of notes, I have given many of 20 them names: Rafiki, Uncle Bert, Icarus, and so on.

This familiarity was not easily won. The textbook instructions for such studies are merely to sit and observe. I wasn't satisfied with this approach; I felt that the gorillas would be doubly suspicious of any alien 25 object that only sat and stared. Instead, I tried to elicit their confidence and curiosity by acting like a gorilla. I imitated their feeding and grooming, and later, when I was surer what they meant, I copied their vocalizations, including some startling deep belching noises. 30

The gorillas have responded favorably, although admittedly these methods are not always dignified. One feels a fool thumping one's chest rhythmically, or sitting about pretending to munch on a stalk of wild celery as though it were the most delectable morsel in the world. 35

Gorillas are the largest of the great apes. A mature male may be six feet tall and weigh 400 pounds or more; his enormous arms can span eight feet. The mountain gorilla's range is limited to a small area of lush wet forests in central Africa. There only a few thousand 40 remain, leading a precarious existence. Part of the territory they occupy has been set aside as parkland, and, theoretically, gorillas are strictly protected. But in fact they are being pushed into ever smaller ranges, chiefly by poachers and Batutsi herdsmen. Unless a 45 better-planned and more-determined effort is made to save the mountain gorilla, it is doomed to extinction within the next two or three decades.

One of the basic steps in saving a threatened species is to learn more about it: its diet, its mating and 50 reproductive processes, its range patterns, its social behavior. I had read of Jane Goodall's studies of chimpanzees and visited her camp in Tanzania's Gombe National Park. In 1967, with help from Dr. Louis Leakey and grants from the National Geographic 55 Society and the Wilkie Brothers Foundation, I began a study of the gorilla.

The study was not without interruptions, one of them quite serious. I began my work in the Congo on the slopes of Mount Mikeno. After only six months of 60 observation, I was forced to leave the country because of political turmoil in Kivo Province. This was a substantial setback, for the gorillas there roamed within a fairly well-protected park system without the constant threat of human intrusion. Thus they were not unduly 65 frightened by my presence, and observations were extremely profitable. After leaving the Congo, I started again, this time in Rwanda. My new camp is near a broad meadow that forms part of the saddle area connecting the Mounts Karisimba, Mikeno and Visoke. 70

Although my old camp was only five miles away, I was to find that the Rwandese gorillas had been so harassed by poachers and cattle grazers that they

rejected all my initial attempts at contact. It was in
Rwanda, after 19 months of work, that the second 75
interruption came. But unlike the first, it was to prove
highly valuable to my study.

Its beginning is still vivid in my mind — a misty
morning in February as I walk up a slippery track of
mud that serves as the main trail between the nearest 80
Rwanda village and my gorilla observation camp at
10,000 feet on Mount Visoke. Behind me, porters carry a
child's playpen, its top boarded over. From the playpen
comes a wailing which grows louder and more piteous
with each step we take. It sounds distressingly like the 85
cry of a human baby.

The chilling fog swirls a tag game in and out of the
great trees; yet the faces of the porters drip sweat after
the four hours of hard climbing since leaving the
Land-Rover at the base of the mountain. Camp is indeed 90
a welcome sight, and the three Africans who comprise
my staff come running out to greet us.

The previous day I had sent them a frantic SOS
asking them to convert one of the two rooms of my cabin
into a forest. To ruin a room by bringing in trees, vines, 95
and other foliage had seemed to them sheer nonsense,
but they were used to my strange requests.

"Chumba tayari," they call now, telling me the room
is all ready. Then, with many screams and orders in
Kinyarwanda, Rwanda's national language, they wedge 100
the playpen through the doors of the cabin and deposit
it amid the trees that sprout between the floorboards.

Now I pry off the top boards of the playpen and
stand back. Two little hands appear from the inside of
the box to grip the edges, and slowly the baby pulls 105
himself up.

How far did you get this time? (If you would like to
read the rest of this article, see the January 1970 issue
of *National Geographic* magazine.) Again, note the line

Measure your comprehension with this quiz.

1. At the time Ms. Fossey wrote this article she had been living with gorillas for:
   - a) 3 months
   - b) 3 years
   - c) 5 years
   - d) 13 years

2. Gorillas are solitary animals, preferring to live alone in caves.
   True or false?

3. Ms. Fossey began her study of mountain gorillas in which country?
   - a) South Africa
   - b) Kenya
   - c) the Congo

4. Ms. Fossey's approach to studying gorillas was to sit in a tree very patiently until they forgot she was there.
   True or false?

5. An adult male gorilla may be six feet tall and weigh 400 pounds or more.
   True or false?

6. The chief threat to the gorillas' existence is:
   - a) poachers
   - b) changing climate
   - c) condominium development

7. One of the basic steps in saving a threatened species is to
   - a) wage a campaign to get protective laws passed
   - b) learn more about it
   - c) employ park rangers to keep poachers away

8. Ms. Fossey had to interrupt her study because of:
   - a) bad weather
   - b) lack of funding
   - c) political turmoil

9. Ms. Fossey sent a message to her staff to have one of the bedrooms:
   - a) cleaned up for unexpected guests
   - b) converted to forest
   - c) baby-proofed

10. She brought the baby gorilla home in a:
   - a) playpen
   - b) Land-Rover
   - c) television box

(Quiz answers are on page 288)

number you stopped on and multiply by nine to calculate your reading speed. Did you do any better?

Comprehending What You Read

The question we hear most from people as they increase their speed is, "How do I know if I'm comprehending what I'm reading?" The answer is: *You actually comprehend as well or better when reading quickly.*

Most people find that they actually remember quite a few details even if they were initially unsure about their comprehension. Here are some additional tips to make sure you get what you need from your reading material. (The key words here are *what you need;* you almost never need to know every word!)

Be an Active Reader

Keep in mind the five W's and an H: Who? When? Where? What? Why? How? Make the text answer your questions as you read. When you ask questions you nudge your mind into a more demanding state, culling ideas from the text as if you were siphoning gasoline from a tank.

Read Ideas, Not Words

The words an author uses are tools to convey ideas, and the only way you can "get the idea" is by reading groups of words in context with one another. When you read one word at a time, your brain has to work much harder to make sense of it. Reading one word at a time is like trying to discover what a boomerang looks like by examining its individual molecules. Instead of reading each word, get the big picture by looking at entire phrases, sentences, and paragraphs.

Involve Your Senses

Use your auditory sense by reading out loud. Read

Tips to Reading Comprehension

■ Be an active reader.

■ Read ideas, not words.

■ Involve your senses.

■ Create interest.

■ Mind Map the material.

the material through fast once, then, if you own the book, involve your kinesthetic and visual senses by underlining important points with a highlighter and drawing pictures in the borders to help you understand key concepts.

Create Interest

It's easier to read material when you're already somewhat familiar with the subject and reading it is going to benefit you in some way. For instance, a friend of mine wanted some in-depth information about elementary school education so she'd be able to help her own children do better in school. She checked out a stack of books from the library. To warm up her mind on the subject, she started by reading *Among Schoolchildren*, a novel about a tough, compassionate fifth-grade teacher in Massachusetts. This book got her so fired up on the subject that she could hardly wait to get to the more informational textbooks afterward. Asking herself, "Why do I need to read this?" she previewed each textbook and was able to eliminate some of them as not appropriate for her needs. Speeding through the ones that *were* appropriate was easy after warming up like this.

Mind Map the Material

After you've read through the material once quickly, make a Mind Map using chapter headings or other topical divisions. Then read it again more thoroughly and fill in the details that are important to remember.

Moving Ahead to Warp Speed

There are basically four different types of reading: regular, skimming, scanning, and warp speed.

Each of the four reading speeds has its own uses.

■ **Regular**
Commonly used for pleasure reading

■ **Skimming**
The way we read telephone books or dictionaries

■ **Scanning**
How newspapers are read

■ **Warp Speed**
Racing through material at high speed with excellent comprehension

Regular . . .

is the relatively slow line-by-line reading that we use for pleasure reading.

Skimming . . .

is done a little more quickly. It's what we do when we're searching for something particular in the text — the way we might read a phone book or dictionary, for example.

Scanning . . .

is used to get an overview of the contents or to preview, the way most of us read the newspaper.

Warp Speed . . .

is the technique of reading through material at great speed with high comprehension.

Knowing how to use all these reading styles is a great advantage to you because it gives you a wide variety of ways to handle your reading. It gives you choices, and the more choices you have, the more power you have to arrange your life in satisfying ways.

Imagine this: You come home from work to find a stack of mail in the mailbox. As you walk into the house, you flip through it, scanning for the "interesting stuff." There are five bills, a letter from your best friend, your monthly subscription to *American Adventure* magazine, a professional journal, and thirteen pieces of apparent junk mail. You put aside the bills to be paid at the end of the month. You skim quickly through the junk mail to make sure nothing of value is hidden in it, find a reimbursement from your insurance company, and throw away the rest. You set the *American Adventure* magazine on your nightstand to read later, then sit down and read the letter from your best friend. You read it twice slowly, savoring every word and conjuring images of your friend as you go. Chuckling over your friend's antics, you change into your jogging clothes. Then,

A reading instructor creates his own success.

Reading instructor Steve Snyder once read fourteen books on a flight between Los Angeles and Sydney, Australia. Using the technique he developed, he generally reads three or four books a night of fiction and nonfiction. His reading speed for this phenomenal feat is about five thousand words per minute. That sounds very fast — and yet he calls this his jogging speed. His sprinting speed is about ten thousand words per minute.

Some people don't believe he could actually be comprehending what he's reading at that speed, so Steve likens speed-reading to skiing. "If you're skiing along nice and slow, you don't really have to pay a lot of attention to what you're doing. Your mind wanders. But if you're speeding down that hill really fast, you have to pay attention." That's why you actually remember the material better when you're going through it quickly, he says.

"You can push yourself to read faster and faster — everybody can. But there is a point where you start to lose comprehension and have to back off," he says.

Some material should also be read very slowly, in his opinion — like poetry, plays, and anything else that is written for the ear rather than the eye.

His career as a speed-reading instructor began at age two when his mother, an avid reader, taught him how to read. When he started first grade, he had already read fourteen hundred books, including the novels of Mark Twain, Jules Verne, and others written at high school level.

At age twelve, his mother allowed him to take a popular speed-reading course, but he was disappointed with the methods taught. "It was hard work and there was no joy in it," Steve recalls, so he decided to develop his own methods. That was when he came up with the techniques he now teaches at Super-Camp. At age fifteen, he began teaching the techniques to his fellow students, who found they could reduce an hour's worth of homework to twenty minutes! Now he teaches seminars worldwide using the same methods he first developed as a boy.

before you leave the house, you take a few minutes to warp read the professional journal and file it away with the rest of your professional papers. It gives you lots of information to mull over, though.

While jogging, the solution to a tough marketing problem comes to you as a result of having read the journal, and you think about how you can present your idea at tomorrow's marketing meeting. Isn't this process a vast improvement over throwing the whole pile on your desk to be gone through later?

You probably already use the first three types of reading — regular, scanning, and skimming. Now let's work on the fourth. To warp read you need to be able to do three things: (1) use your peripheral vision, (2) move your eyes quickly down a page of text, and (3) turn pages quickly. Add these skills to your ability to focus your attention and be an active participant, and you'll soon find your speed and comprehension increasing dramatically.

Increasing Your Peripheral Vision

When you go to an optometrist for an eye exam, the doctor tests your peripheral vision with a machine that is activated when you look straight ahead into a large black bowl. Small lights, like little stars, blink on and off in various places around the bowl, and you push a button every time you see a light. The lights blink farther and farther from the center of the bowl, where your eyes are focused. Some you don't see there at all, because they're outside your peripheral vision.

Try the test to the right and determine your peripheral vision. Most people can see things at a 45-degree angle from center, and some can see even farther — perhaps up to 90 degrees or so.

In reading, a wider peripheral vision translates into the ability to take in more information at one time. You read faster when you take in complete phrases at a glance. Best of all, you can train yourself to have a

Improving peripheral vision enables you to take in more information at each glance.

To discover your peripheral vision, take this simple test:

- Look straight ahead at an object.

- Hold your arms out to your sides with your index fingers pointing upward.

- Move your arms slowly inward until you can see your fingers.

- Notice your range of sight while looking straight ahead.

wider and wider peripheral vision.

Steve Snyder, a reading instructor at many Super-Camps, teaches students to improve their peripheral vision with a "tri-focus" exercise, which also breaks the habit of focusing on each word individually and corrects a habit of fixating on individual words. Simply break each line of text into thirds. As you read, focus on the left third, followed by the center third, and finally the last third, taking in each group of words with your peripheral vision rather than looking at each word. Here is an example:

In the night sky / was a very bright star / that everyone saw.

Steve has a "magic book" to help students practice this reading technique. The first thing students notice about this book is that it has no words in it. Instead, each page is filled with symbols that look like this:

_____ * _____   _____ * _____   _____ * _____

To "read" the magic book, you simply focus on the left third (with the center of your focus on the star), then the center third, then the right third. As you imagine reading page after page of this exercise, you begin to see that this book is not about *what* to read, it's about *how* to read.

As you move your eyes, the most important aspect of this exercise is to imagine how magnificent this book is, and how wonderful it is to read much faster, with far greater comprehension. Get into a rhythm, counting 1,2,3 — 1,2,3 . . . or use a metronome if you have one.

Now practice reading the page at right from the "magic book."

Practice this exercise for twenty to forty seconds several times each day. Then try using this tri-focus method to read a "regular book." Mentally break each line in your book into thirds, as we did in the sentence about the bright star, then make your eyes jump to the

To use Steve Snyder's tri-focus technique, scan the left third, center third, and right third, focusing on the stars.

middle of each third, seeing peripherally the words on the edges. (For practice exercises like this, it's always best to use reading materials that are interesting to you.)

Another way to improve your peripheral vision is to try reading a page while focusing your eyes on the white between the lines rather than on the actual words. This is called a "soft focus" and has the additional advantage of being easy on your eyes.

Page-Turning Techniques

Think about this: You can read only as fast as you can turn pages. Yes, to be a warp reader you have to be able to turn the pages at warp speed! Here are some exercises in page-turning that we teach at SuperCamp.

With your left hand holding the book open at the top center or left border, use your right hand to brush first the left then the right page vertically top to bottom. As you come to the bottom of the right page, reach over with your left hand and turn the page, as in the diagram on the page at right.

A variation of this is to move your right hand in a U pattern from left to right, as shown at right.

You may find this easier if at first you turn the book upside down. That way you won't be tempted to slow down or stop when your eyes snag on a word or phrase. Timing yourself for one minute, try turning one hundred pages with your left hand while brushing each one or making a U with your right. Then turn the book right side up and do it for another minute.

Hyperscan to Increase Eye Speed

I've already mentioned how useful moving your index finger line by line can be in increasing your reading speed. Now, here are some more specific patterns you can try to help you increase even more the speed at which your eyes move through the pages.

Being able to rapidly turn pages is a key to improving reading speed.

While turning pages with your left hand, use one of the patterns with your right to guide your eyes.

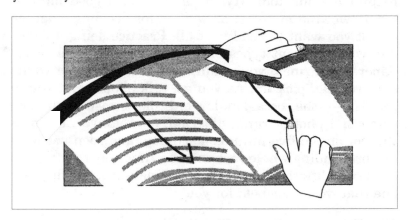

Brush Method

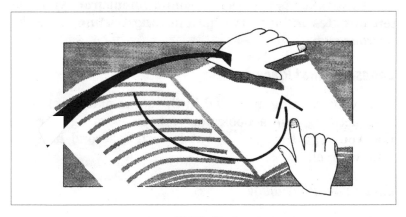

U Method

Pick up a book right now, any book. Using your finger(s) to guide your eyes, move down each page using one of the patterns.

As you read, have your eyes follow your finger(s) moving quickly down the page. Don't try to read every word. Think about what you're seeing. Think about any pictures or charts. Ask yourself questions as you scan. Try to see the whole concepts being presented on the page.

This technique is called hyperscanning, and it is a helpful reading tool. Hyperscanning is a good method for previewing material as well as for deciding whether or not you want to read it at all. Practice doing it every day with different types of reading material: the newspaper, magazines, your mail, class assignments, whatever you can pick up. As you go, talk about what you're seeing — the occasional word or phrase your eye catches, a photo, graph, diagram, or whatever. Practice this for one to five minutes each day, and soon you'll be comprehending whole sections at a time.

Try a different pattern each time until you find the one that works the best for you.

Ten Minutes a Day to Put It All Together

All it takes is a personal commitment from you and ten minutes a day. Try the following routine, or make up your own.

Choose a Quiet Place . . .

to do your reading and read in the same place each day. In practicing, use a book you've been wanting to read. Use your egg timer or a watch with a second hand to time yourself.

Check Your Physiology

Sit on the edge of your seat with your book propped on the desk or table in front of you, about fourteen

An additional pattern you can use is the Slalom Method, which is like skiing down the page.

inches away from your eyes. Make sure you're sitting up straight, feet flat on the ground. Take a moment to calm your mind and relax your body.

Preview the Book for One Minute

Look at the title, contents page, chapter titles, headings and subheadings, pictures, photos, graphs, and chapter summaries. Ask yourself as you preview, "What's this book about?"

Turn the Book Upside Down

Practice turning the pages as fast as you can for one minute, running your finger down each page. Talk out loud about what you're seeing as you turn the pages. After a minute, stop and see how many pages you turned. Now do it again for another minute and see if you can increase your speed. Aim for one hundred pages per minute or more.

Now Turn the Book Right Side Up

Look up at the ceiling and think of your peaceful place, take a deep breath, then look down at your book and begin reading. Turn the pages quickly, and use your finger or other pointer to move your eyes down the page using one of the hyperscan patterns. Ask questions as you go, like "What is the material about? What does the author say about it? How or why is this true? So what? Why is it important?"

Pretend you have an audience who is wondering what you're reading, and give them impressions as they come to you. It might sound something like this: "Well, now what can this book be about? I see a color diagram of clouds and ocean with arrows and a photo of an iceberg and lots of color-coded maps. Could it be something about the weather? Yes, I see this is about the water cycle of the earth. Now, I wonder what the author has to say about it. . . . "

To improve speed and comprehension, follow this routine for ten minutes a day.

- Choose a quiet place to read.

- Check your physiology.

- Preview the book for one minute.

- Turn the book upside down and practice turning pages.

- Turn the book right side up.

- Look up at the ceiling and think of a peaceful place.

- Take a deep breath.

- Look down and begin reading.

- Turn pages correctly.

- Use your finger(s) and practice a pattern.

- Ask yourself questions as you read.

Keep moving ahead smoothly, remembering to focus on phrases instead of individual words. Use a different pattern every day until you discover your personal preference.

Eyes Tired?

When your eyes get tired, try this simple fatigue and stress reliever. First, rub your hands together briskly for a few moments, then close your eyes and cup your hands over them, holding your fingers together so that no light penetrates. Imagine you are in a beautiful, peaceful place — like a forest where the air is fresh and cool and trees sway in the wind. Allow your eyes to drift upward for a few moments as you imagine this peaceful, relaxing place. Follow the motion of the trees back and forth, up and down, with your eyes; this is good for relieving tension in the muscles around your eyeballs. Tell yourself what a good job you're doing, that it's easy to be a good reader, and that your speed and comprehension are incredible! Then slowly take your hands away and open your eyes.

The Final Test

You should be ready to use your new techniques and take the last reading test to see how much you've improved.

If you'd like to practice a little, do that right now, for just about ten minutes. If not, get right to it.

Again, check your physiology: sit up straight on the edge of your seat, feet flat on the floor, book propped in front of you. Take a moment to calm your mind and focus your concentration. Set your timer for one minute, look up for a minute, then down at the page and begin.

Education's Ecstasy Explosion

by Lyelle Palmer

Creating Joy in the Classroom Through Suggestion and Cycle

Accelerative learning and teaching is the 5
orchestration of classroom practice to recondition
students into a positive mental and physiological
learning state through many means of obvious and
subtle suggestion. The accelerative teacher creates a
classroom that produces a positive inner self which 10
supports easy and creative action abilities in the
student. Obviously, students succeed at a much higher
(accelerative) rate and the classroom becomes a fun
place besides. Teachers become energized and inspired
because they suddenly recognize that there is no place 15
in the whole world that offers as much possibility for
excitement on a day-to-day basis as a class of students
(at any age). Once teachers have experienced the
vibrant and colorful success of the positive whole-brain
approach, they would never consider going back to the 20
black-and-white life of the conventional classroom.

Preparatory Phase

Specific activities of the accelerative classroom occur
in three distinct segments. First is the *preparatory
phase,* in which the students' external and internal 25
environments are prepared for learning to take place
quickly and easily. In order to decondition/recondition
the students, the classroom is organized differently from
a typical classroom. Chairs are arranged in a semicircle
so that students can make eye contact with each other 30
as a cozy group. The room is orderly and pleasant, free
of fatiguing clutter. Flowers and/or pictures (real art)
create an uplifting ambiance. The total lesson is placed

on colorful, teacher-made wall posters; three-dimensional letters, shaded letters, and a picture as a 35 mnemonic device are included in each poster. Positive affirmations are placed on the walls, on overhead wires or string, or on desks. Calming classical music is played as the students enter the class.

The class begins with a few minutes of physical 40 activity to loosen up muscles. (Back rubbing is also good. Would you be tardy to a class where you get a back rub during the first minute?) Next, body relaxation and positive revisualization of past success put the students in a peak performance mental state and 45 relaxed attentiveness to whatever takes place in the class. Mental affirmations and positive suggestions are given to the students, such as, "Today, you'll be interested to know the next segment of our course and how it expands your knowledge and insights of 50 everything we've covered so far. It's amazing how quickly the creative connections begin to develop at about this time in this content."

Material Presentation Phase

The second phase is the *material presentation phase,* 55 which takes place energetically and dramatically (often with dramatic classical music as a background). All teaching is considered foreign-language instruction in this phase, and new terms and concepts are explained as an expanded decoding exercise and are then related 60 to previously learned material. The format may contain restating all material three or more times incidentally. The presentation may be brief or extended; questions and drill are avoided throughout, although occasionally students may be directed to respond with directives: 65 "Tell your neighbor as many types of preparation-phase components to an accelerative learning class as you can recall" (rather than, "Can you remember all of the preparation-phase components?").

In order to engage attention fully with students of 70
any age, the presentation may use puppets and
dramatic, flamboyant teacher action. Teachers learn to
intone as they speak so that the subdominant language
hemisphere of the brain is engaged. Positive words and
modality-engaging words and intonations activate the 75
brains of students with visual, auditory, and
kinesthetic/tactile learning preferences or styles.
Students close their eyes and visualize content or link
outrageous visual mnemonics to the content. Metaphors
and analogies create easily recalled images; songs are 80
often created as well. A script written by the teachers
puts the content into a role-playing or dramatic episode.
Cards distributed personify concepts or terms ("I am
input; I travel up the affector nerves into the brain from
sensors such as the eyes, ears, skin, nose, tongue, or 85
muscle"). Students become objects as a group (i.e. each
student becomes one of the various components of a
class lesson plan). The teacher demonstrates, shows,
tells, touches, moves, and reviews. Students also
present within a small group or to the entire class, so 90
that confident peer teaching and cooperative learning
take place. Standing and moving are purposely built
into lessons.

A passive review often consolidates information the
brain has received. Here we must note that the brain 95
records every moment of experience at all times: it can't
not record, learn, absorb, receive. The brain receives
best when fully focused, with no distractions (threat),
and when information is presented in the best modality
or all modalities. In an eyes-closed, relaxed, high blood 100
carbon dioxide state, the brain cells fire most efficiently
during the calm mind review. Listening to the teacher
review lesson content with relaxed attentiveness is an
essential, powerful, pleasant, and imaginative activity
to which student look forward as a positive benefit of 105
accelerated learning. The review includes visualizing
content from the active first presentation, and it may

include other reminders of previously learned material, such as the script, the song, and the movements. After effortlessly taking in the passive review, the student 110 may briefly look over (not study or "try" to learn) the content before going to sleep that night. This allows the student's mind to consolidate the material overnight.

Activation and Elaboration Phase

The final phase, the *activation and elaboration* 115 *phase,* allows students to use learned material in simulations or games, including role playing, assuming identities, and using self-corrected, nongraded quizzes. Corrections are made indirectly, never identifying the student who made the error, but gently reteaching to 120 the entire class to clarify the content. Eventually, graded quizzes are used occasionally, after students have mastered the material and have confidence in their knowledge or skill. Final examinations have been known to consist of group projects in which students 125 construct a set of materials, including songs, skits with scripts, wall charts (visuals), and simulations. Follow-up tests on knowledge several months later have shown a remarkable retention rate for class content that goes far beyond conventional teaching and learning. 130

Research and Implications

Data gathered by teachers and researchers have been reported in research journals for the past fifteen years. A number of masters' theses and doctoral dissertations have been completed on accelerative 135 learning topics. Several literature reviews of accelerative learning have indicated a mass of evidence for effectiveness of these humane classroom practices. Two meta-analyses of research findings in accelerative learning have been conducted by educational 140 researchers. One of them shows highly significant effects in foreign language teaching, and the other indicated that some classes of special needs students were providing a rate of learning two to four times that of normal children! 145

Beyond the proven academic results, the "natural high" produced by accelerative learning has far-reaching implications. At present, drug usage is a major problem with our youth. Accelerative learning teachers observe 150 that, if students receive an ecstatic high from successful learning in a pleasant, fun, socially comfortable, and caring environment, then drugs have no allure. In contrast, if students never feel good or normal unless drugs are being used, then drugs will be highly desired. 155 Perhaps a fundamental way of pre-empting the desire for drugs is to give students positive experiences that are valued and readily available on a personal initiative basis. The many benefits of the accelerative learning approach of consistently positive learning experiences 160 may be more than just a nice idea. Just possibly, these positive benefits may be an absolute necessity for the kind of world we want to build, and into which we want our children and grandchildren to be born. Choosing a positive, accelerative, natural high produces a high level 165 of productivity and caring, independence, and extraordinary creativity. Students see that they can take personal responsibility for positive choices in life and that, instead of being helpless victims of life, they have abundant opportunities to choose heroism. 170

Score yourself for speed, then answer the questions on the following pages to check your comprehension. You may be surprised at how much you remember! If you finished in less than a minute, you are doing fantastic! You may want to write your own book.

Test your reading comprehension with this quiz:

1. A goal of accelerative teaching is to create a positive inner-self.

   True or false?

2. In an accelerative learning classroom, chairs are arranged:
   a) so that every student can see out the window.
   b) in a semicircle so students can make eye contact.
   c) in groups of four to six.

3. Flowers, art, posters, and signs are considered distracting and thus are never used in an accelerative learning classroom.

   True or false?

4. To begin a class, Lyelle Palmer suggests the use of:
   a) a period of silence.
   b) exercise and back rubs.
   c) a quick energy snack.

5. In the *material presentation stage,* information is presented:
   a) energetically and dramatically.
   b) with background music.
   c) with colorful posters.
   d) all of the above.

. . . test continues on next page ☞

6. In order to make sure all types of learners can understand the material, the teacher shows, tells, touches, moves, and reviews.

    True or false?

7. After presenting the material, the teacher should then drill the students to make sure they understood it correctly.

    True or false?

8. An essential program of the review session is:
    a) relaxed attentiveness.
    b) flash cards.
    c) handouts about the subject.

9. To help students learn the material, they are encouraged to participate in role-playing, singing songs about the subject, playing games, and closing their eyes to visualize the concepts.

    True or false?

10. Accelerative learning teachers have observed that if students receive an ecstatic high from successful learning in a pleasant, fun, socially comfortable, and caring environment, then drugs have no allure.

    True or false?

Second Test Answers: 1. T 2. b 3. F 4. b 5. d
6. T 7. F 8. a 9. T 10. T

First Quiz Answers: 1. b 2. F 3. c 4. F 5. T
6. a 7. b 8. c 9. b 10. a

I Know I Know

✔ Check the box if you understand the concept:

☐ I know the correct physiology for reading.

☐ I know how to relax and focus my attention.

☐ I know how to preview my reading material.

☐ I know how to be an active reader and read ideas, not words.

☐ I know how to create interest in my reading.

☐ I know the tri-focus exercise.

☐ I know three patterns to use for hyperscanning:

1 _____

2 _____

3 _____

☐ I know a page-turning technique to increase my reading speed. I turn _____ pages per minute.

☐ I know I am a powerful reader.

11

Thinking Logically, Thinking Creatively

Why should you read this chapter?

☑ Maximize creative problem-solving processes.

☑ Allow your right brain to work on challenging situations.

☑ Understand the role of personal paradigms in creative processes.

☑ Learn how brainstorming can provide innovative solutions for many problems.

☑ Discover success in "Outcome Thinking."

A creative person is curious, experimental, adventurous, playful, intuitive — and *you* have the potential to be this creative person. In this chapter you will delve into your creative mind and find new ways to use these traits to help you in your adult endeavors.

On a scale of one to ten, how creative are you? Steve Curtis, a businessman and creativity expert, always asks prospective employees this question. He hires the person who answers, "Ten."

When asked to explain this policy, he says "We're all born with creativity, and if you *believe* you're a creative person you will find ways to creatively cope with day-to-day problems on the job and in your personal life. That's the kind of person I want to work with."

In our society, we tend to view certain kinds of people, like artists, scientists, and inventors, as being somehow mysterious — just because they're "creative." Yet we *all* have the ability to be creative thinkers and problem solvers. What it takes is an inquisitive mind, a willingness to take risks, and the drive to make things work — three qualities that are available to anyone.

For all the attention creativity gets, most creativity is manifested quite humbly. It goes pretty much unnoticed by civilization, yet in small ways makes life a little more pleasant. I'm talking about creative accomplishments like discovering a way to keep ants out of the dog's dish, or decorating a room without spending lots of money, or inventing a way to recycle your bathwater to water your plants, or experimenting with different food combinations to come up with a tasty new recipe.

Take a few moments to remember a few situations in which *you* reached a goal or solved a problem when the situation seemed hopeless. You were stumped, or trapped, or caught in a bind you'd never been in before. But you found a way. That's *creativity*.

Maybe you've even had the experience of inventing a solution to some particularly irritating problem and later finding your invention in a store — which means

A creative person is curious, experimental, playful, and intuitive; you have the potential to be this creative person.

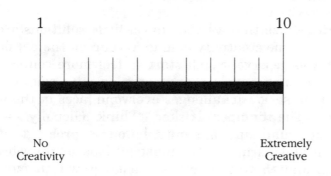

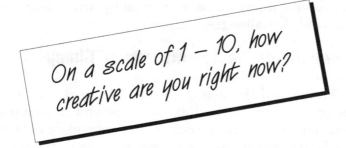

some entrepreneurial person just took your idea a few steps further.

If you think about each of your own examples, you'll discover that the solutions almost always came from knowledge you already had, or from knowledge borrowed from other people — thus the old adage, "There's nothing new under the sun." There are only new versions and combinations. Even ideas considered "revolutionary" stem from a foundation of established knowledge. What creative people usually do with that knowledge, however, is take the leap that allows them to see it in ways it has never been seen before. (This usually involves a paradigm shift, which I'll discuss later.)

Recognize that all your novel little solutions are the result of true creativity, and give yourself the pat on the back you deserve. You'll start to feel more confident in your ability to explore and come up with solutions for the more serious challenges everyone faces in the world today. The bumper sticker "Think Globally — Act Locally" sums up what must be our approach to world health and harmony. We must all look at the world at large, and then each of us must act within our own sphere of influence in ways that are thoughtful, creative, and forward-looking. To do this we must be able to absorb new information and come up with solutions for a myriad of challenges.

Information: The Raw Material of Change

The world is changing at an accelerating rate, largely because of the huge volume and availability of information — it is *abundant* and extremely *accessible*. The faster information gets out into the world and into the minds of people, the faster people absorb it and combine and recombine it to create more new concepts, theories, facts, and inventions. This produces an ever-accelerating rate of change in the world.

Creative people use knowledge we all have and make the leap that allows them to see things in new ways.

This has tremendous implications for us as business people, educators, students, parents, and responsible world citizens. Old patterns of thought and passive adaptation might be enough to let us drift along with the flow, but to be truly effective and fulfilled, we need to ride the crest of this postindustrial information wave. We need thinking skills that allow us to assimilate new information for use in our homes, businesses and schools. We need to creatively adapt that information to our lives for positive outcomes.

In her book *Developing a 21st Century Mind*, educator Marsha Sinetar describes a quality of "creative adaptiveness" that she believes is desirable in all aspects of being human — from personal growth and enrichment, to business and career, to parenting, and family life. Creative adaptiveness can look like play and in fact *is* playful, yet it involves a way of thinking that's logical and sequential as well as intuitive and deeply personal — in short, it's a whole-brain thought process for effective problem-solving.

A Look at Problem-Solving Processes

In recent years, we seem to be confronted at every turn with new terms for problem-solving processes. Here are a few of those terms, with some simple definitions.

Vertical Thinking

A process of moving step by step toward your goal, as if you were climbing a ladder.

Lateral Thinking

Looking at your problem from several new angles, as if jumping from one ladder to another.

Information is abundant and extremely accessible, producing an ever-accelerating rate of change in the world.

"Ride the crest" of the information wave.

Critical Thinking

Exercising or involving careful judgment or evaluation, such as judging the feasibility of an idea or product.

Analytical Thinking

A process of breaking your problem or idea into parts, examining each part to see how it fits together with the others, and exploring how these parts can be recombined in new ways.

Strategic Thinking

Developing a specific strategy for the planning and direction of large-scale operations by looking at the project from all possible angles.

Outcome Thinking

Attacking a task from the perspective of the desired solution.

Creative Thinking

The so-called "lightbulb" effect that occurs when you rearrange existing facts and come up with new insight on the subject. (This almost always involves lateral thinking.)

All these kinds of thinking might be categorized as right-brain or left-brain processes, in which case, we would find lateral, outcome, and creative thinking on the intuitive right, and vertical, critical, strategic, and analytical thinking on the logical left. In truth, though, there is a lot of overlap. Problem-solving, like any intellectual activity, is a combination of creative and logical thought. And true creative problem solvers use a combination of all these processes. It's important to remember

Problem-solving is a combination of logical and creative thought.

Use both left-brain and right-brain thinking processes:

- Vertical
- Critical
- Strategic
- Analytical

- Lateral
- Outcome
- Creative

that creativity goes beyond that initial creative spark to the actual execution of the idea.

From beginning to end, creative problem-solving flows through these specific stages:

Preparation

You define the problem, goal, or challenge.

Incubation

You digest the facts and allow things to stew in your mind.

Illumination

Ideas come bubbling to the surface.

Verification

You decide if the solution really solves the problem.

Application

You take steps to follow through with the solution.

Laying the Foundation

All great creative endeavors — from the break-through theories of an Einstein, to a great advertising campaign, to an ambitious self-improvement program — must have a solid foundation. Here's how you lay that foundation.

You start with your own current knowledge and that of other people, and you build from there. When you define a goal, you are using your logical, methodical left brain to create a map for your right brain to follow during the incubation and illumination phases, which come later. And although research is not usually thought of as a creative activity, to guarantee success for your endeavor, you must be sure your research is thorough.

The creative process flows through five stages.

■ **Preparation**   Defining the problem, goal, or challenge.

■ **Incubation**   Digesting the facts and stewing them in your mind.

■ **Illumination**   Bubbling to the surface, ideas are produced.

■ **Verification**   Deciding if the solution really solves the problem.

■ **Application**   Taking the steps to follow through with the solution.

Collect books and articles on your subject, then read and file them. Find out who the authorities on your subject are and talk to them. Know what the benefits will be when the solution or goal is achieved, as well as what some of the obstacles might be to accomplishing the goal. Then state your problem or goal in precise, detailed language. Throughout this phase, remember to tell yourself:

I am a high performer!

Believe that you're capable of finding a solution. Research has proven that people are much more likely to accept the fact that a problem exists if they believe in their ability to find solutions. And accepting the existence of a problem is the first step in solving it.

When all the facts are in, you enter the incubation or "ruminating" phase — going over the facts casually and slowly in your mind. This is a right-brain stage which people often cut short, just because they mistake it for "doing nothing." Since you live in a left-brain society where "doing nothing" is frowned upon, the critic in you steps in to reprimand and prod you to action, thus stifling your creativity.

Fortunately, now that you know how this happens, you can prevent it by consciously giving yourself permission to "do nothing" until incubation gives way to illumination.

For the incubation phase, find your best "rambling thought" activity. This might be some physical activity that doesn't require a lot of concentration, such as swimming, walking, or pulling weeds. This activity opens the door to your mind and allows rambling thoughts to pour in. Other such activities are listening to music, daydreaming, taking a bath, and driving on the freeway.

Since there isn't always a clear point when incubation ends and illumination begins, you'll want to keep a small notebook in your pocket or car to capture your ideas as soon as they start occurring.

Give yourself permission to "do nothing" until incubation gives way to illumination.

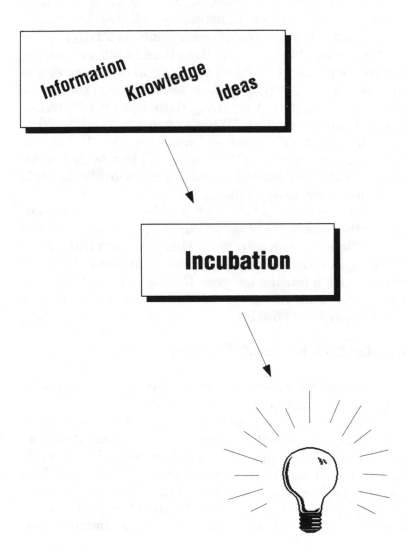

In the next few pages, you'll learn about outcome thinking, paradigm shifts, and brainstorming, which are all ways of moving toward solutions.

What Does It Feel Like to Live in Your Solution?

"Problem thinking" can be negative. Questions like "What's wrong?" "Who messed up?" "Why is this happening to me?" "Who is to blame?" — all dwell on what's wrong and can drain you of energy and creativity.

"Outcome thinking," on the other hand, is positive. It's the opposite of problem thinking and will move you in the right direction rather than letting you muck around in negative thoughts. With outcome thinking, you ask questions like "What's in my control?" "What can I do about it?" "What will mobilize me?" "What will motivate and excite me?" "How can I change this situation?" Outcome thinking changes energy-draining problems into energizing goals.

Think *solution* rather than *problem,* and align yourself with success. In other words, imagine how it would feel to "live in your solution." This is a powerful way of arriving at *ways* to make the solution come about. It also creates a tension between the problem and the solution. This tension has a natural tendency to resolve itself toward the positive.

Exercises in Outcome Thinking

Here is an outcome thinking exercise you can try for defining and attaining personal goals.

Imagine it's five years from now, and you've done everything you hoped to have done with your life so far. You're healthy, happy, successful in your chosen activity, and well balanced in all aspects of your life. Now you're applying for a position that will move you into even greater fulfillment and financial security. However, it's been several years since you updated your

Outcome thinking changes energy-draining problems into energizing goals.

Think solution rather than problem by asking yourself these questions:

- What's in my control?

- What can I do about it?

- What will mobilize me?

- What will motivate and excite me?

resume. *Write the resume that describes you as this balanced and successful person.*

As an alternative, imagine you're such an interesting, dynamic pioneer of a person, that a feature writer from the newspaper in the nearest large city came and interviewed you for a profile story. *Write the story you'd like to see about yourself.* Go so far as to imagine the photos that would accompany the article, and write captions for them.

These activities are fun, and they're also perfect ways to use outcome thinking. You'll find that once you can visualize yourself as the person you want to be with great clarity, you'll naturally start moving in that direction. The "power of vision" is a very effective motivator for change. Social scientists over the years have noted that significant action is always preceded by a significant vision, for individuals as well as for nations.

Paradigm Shifts, or "Changing Ladders"

Creative thinking isn't a matter of working harder — it's a matter of thinking differently. Many times, this involves a lateral thinking phenomenon called a "paradigm shift." (Remember the concept of "changing ladders" in lateral thinking?)

A paradigm is a set of rules we use for evaluating information and incorporating it into our lives. Everyone has their own paradigms based on what their life experience has been. These paradigms are useful to you in many ways. But they can also be limiting. They can hide opportunity from you, simply because your frame of reference doesn't acknowledge the existence of the opportunity.

A perfect example of this is the story of how the Swiss went from being the world's leader in watch manufacturing to a minor player in just a decade. A Swiss researcher was the inventor of the quartz watch, but his idea was rejected by the watch manufacturer he worked

By visualizing with great clarity the person you want to become, you'll naturally start moving in that direction.

1

Your Resume

Write a resume that describes you as a balanced and successful person.

- your general information
- your education
- your work history
- your membership in groups and clubs
- your successes
- your references

2

Daily News

Your Photo	*Your Headline and Story*

Caption

This is a story about you as an interest- ing, dyna- mic pioneer	of a person. A feature writer from the news- paper in the	nearest large city came and inter- viewed you for a profile	story. Write the story you'd like to see about your- self.	Be as creative and imagin- ative as you can be. Have fun!

for because watches "just weren't made that way." So blind were the Swiss to the benefits of this new concept that they didn't even bother to patent the idea. The researcher took his quartz watch to a trade show shortly afterward, and there it was discovered by Seiko and Texas Instruments. They lacked the limiting paradigms of the Swiss and started manufacturing it immediately.

Living through a paradigm is like always looking through the same window and thus always seeing the same little segment of the world. You could go through your whole life looking through the same window and live a fine life. After all, having some kind of window is better than not having one.

Entire vistas may be completely obscured, but if you've never seen them you have no reason to think of them or feel deprived, do you? A "paradigm shift" is like suddenly discovering a new window through which all kinds of new things are visible — or through which old things can be seen in different ways. And once you know there's more than one window, it becomes easy to imagine that there might be even more windows someplace else. Somewhere in your mind a light flicks on . . . and then another and another. Paradigm shifts allow you to think outside your current patterns of thought and thus come up with fresh new solutions.

Talking about paradigm shifts is easier than making them, however. Although they sometimes occur in a flash of insight (the lightbulb effect), more often it's a matter of shuffling around the problem and looking at it from all angles. Most important, you have to be aware that paradigms exist in order to think about looking outside of them.

Let's return to the ladder metaphor. Imagine yourself climbing a ladder, step by step toward a solution. Suddenly, you discover that the ladder is leaning against the wrong wall! Sometimes a problem is a problem only because you're viewing it from only one angle. Looked at from another, the solution becomes so obvious

Paradigm: A set of rules we use for evaluating information and incorporating it into our lives.

*A "paradigm shift" is like suddenly discovering
a new window to look through.*

that it's no longer a problem.

Here's an example from Eugene Raudsepp's *Creative Growth Games*. Look at the sketch on the right, and imagine that you're the person shown standing in this room. You've been given the task of tying together the two strings suspended from the ceiling. The strings are located so that you can't reach one string with your outstretched hand while holding the second in your other hand. The room is totally bare, and you have only the resources you would normally have in your pocket or purse. How do you solve the problem? Please take five minutes to think about it now before reading on to discover an answer. (Notice that I said "an" answer and not "the" answer; there are quite possibly more than one.)

Most people state the problem as "How can I get to the second string?" then spend a lot of effort trying to find a way of making one of the strings longer. But the "givens" of this problem make such a solution impossible. In other words, the ladder is leaning on the wrong wall. If, however, you define the problem as "How can the string and I get together?" another sort of solution may occur to you. If you tie a small object — say, a key or a ring — to the end of one string and swing it like a pendulum, then you can grab it while still holding the end of the second string in the other hand.

Did you see the shift? The next time you're faced with a challenging situation, remember to look at it from all angles and redefine the problem if necessary. It may just be that all you need is a shift in your viewpoint.

Brainstorming

Brainstorming is a problem-solving technique that can be used by an individual or a group. It involves recording spontaneous ideas as they occur in a nonjudg-

When faced with a challenging situation, look at it from all angles and redefine the problem if necessary.

How can you tie the two strings together?

mental fashion. It's based on the premise that to get truly great ideas you must have lots of ideas to choose from. This is similar to the photographer's theory that if you snap an entire roll of film, you'll probably end up with a couple of good photos along with the many inevitable bad ones. Trouble is, while you're snapping, you don't know which ones will be good and which won't. That's why you have to snap a lot and not judge them until later.

Brainstorming is especially effective in groups because of the cumulative effect of each mind being stimulated by the creativity of all the others. When most of us think of brainstorming, we picture a conference room with people seated around a table, tossing ideas to a facilitator who writes them down on a blackboard or flipchart. You can also brainstorm by yourself and record your ideas using the clustering method described earlier in this book. Clustering allows you to see connections between ideas and piggyback ideas on each other.

I've found that large sheets of plain paper work well for brainstorm clustering. Make sure your problem or subject is well defined, then write down a key word or phrase in the center of your paper and circle it. Then let the ideas start to flow. As each one occurs, jot it down, circle it, and connect it to the center subject or to the circled thought that triggered it.

It's important to *accept all ideas as good ideas,* no matter how far-fetched they are. In fact, you should seek the far-fetched, because true innovation often looks impossible at first glance.

Go for quantity! When you think you've listed everything you can think of, make yourself come up with five more ideas. Force your brain into new areas. It's good exercise and may help you to think of a solution that nobody else ever thought of before.

In brainstorming, accept all ideas as good ideas, no matter how farfetched they may seem.

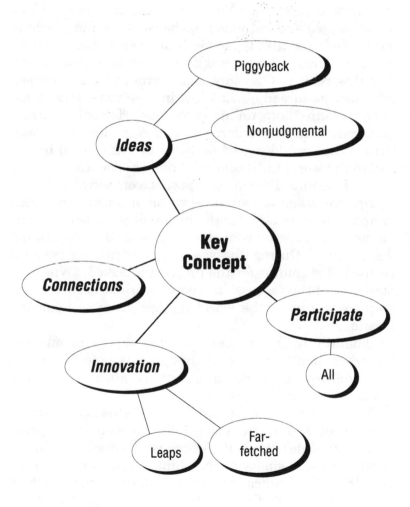

Brainstorming the Future

Envisioning the future is one of the most important uses for creativity. The present is the raw material from which the future will be built. Projecting what will happen, predicting what variables will shape the future — this is the ultimate exercise in creative thought.

Five hundred years ago, the great Italian artist and visionary Leonardo da Vinci drew sketches of his ideas for airplanes and automobiles, helicopters and machine guns. We know that these ideas have since become reality, but we don't know exactly how he was able to *predict* this reality. Our only explanation is that he used information already available in his time and made "mental leaps" into unknown realms. He took information, combined it, reordered it, and came up with possibilities that would not be accepted or understood by the rest of the world until centuries after his death.

At Learning Forum, the parent company of Super-Camp, we stage an annual "vision meeting" in which company leaders plan for the future of the business. The theme of a recent vision meeting was "Brainstorming the Future." During the session, participants posed a number of scenarios for the future and asked, "What if?" Step One of the process focused on world situations, and Step Two brought the world picture home to Learning Forum.

The key to this process was that every member of the group had to accept all thoughts as potential realities and ask open-ended questions about how each would affect our business.

What would happen, for instance, if school systems throughout the entire United States went to a year-round schedule? What if the crisis in education finally affected U.S. business to the point that businesses took over the job of educating our populace? What if UFOs arrived en masse? (Don't scoff — it *could* happen.) What if information could be downloaded, computerlike, into

Creative anticipation of the future is what transforms ordinary businesses into leading-edge pioneers.

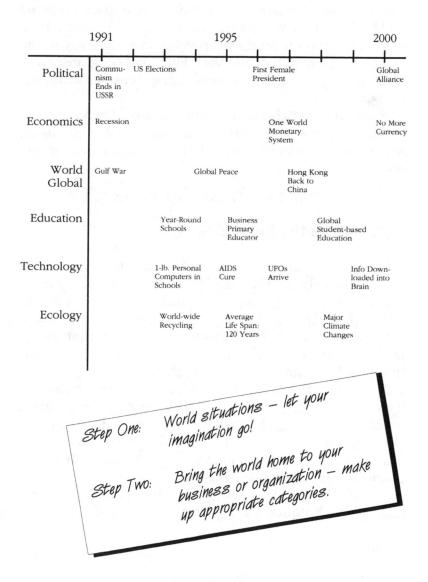

	1991		1995		2000
Political	Commu- nism Ends in USSR	US Elections	First Female President		Global Alliance
Economics	Recession		One World Monetary System		No More Currency
World Global	Gulf War	Global Peace	Hong Kong Back to China		
Education		Year-Round Schools	Business Primary Educator	Global Student-based Education	
Technology		1-lb. Personal Computers in Schools	AIDS Cure	UFOs Arrive	Info Down- loaded into Brain
Ecology		World-wide Recycling	Average Life Span: 120 Years	Major Climate Changes	

Step One: World situations — let your imagination go!

Step Two: Bring the world home to your business or organization — make up appropriate categories.

our brains? What if the human lifespan were extended to 120 years? What if there were space-station colonies, and all education were transmitted by satellite? What if car phones become as widely used as televisions?

Some scenarios seemed so imminently possible that we had to amend our ten-year strategic plan to accommodate them. Others were so far-fetched, they made us all laugh. Yet each of us was aware that the most outrageous ideas might produce a revolution in the way we do business. (Remember, not very long ago, computers, fax machines, and portable telephones were outrageous ideas.)

Creative anticipation of the future is what transforms ordinary businesses into leading-edge pioneers. And if there's a simple formula for becoming such a pioneer, it could be:

The Present + Outrageous Ideas = The Future

"Drawing on the Right Side of Your Brain"

Ned Herrmann is an expert on how the brain functions creatively, and he has designed and led many creative thinking workshops for companies such as GE, Shell, IBM, Du Pont, and AT&T. When he was doing research for his first workshop, he found that many business executives could be convinced they were creative people if they could be taught to draw. Since Ned believed that the first step in enhancing people's creativity was to convince them that they *were* in fact creative people, he got together with Betty Edwards, author of *Drawing on the Right Side of the Brain*, to show a left-brain group of nuclear engineers how to draw. It was a phenomenally successful experiment.

Using the mental aspect of "seeing" rather than traditional techniques of art instruction, you, too, can draw!

Leading edge pioneers create the future by pursuing all ideas and keeping their vision in focus.

The Present
+
Outrageous Ideas
=
The Future

Directions for Drawing Exercise

Find a blank, unlined piece of paper and a pencil. Put on some relaxing baroque music, such as that composed by Pachebel, Handel, or Corelli. Now look at the drawing on the page to the right for a moment. (Don't turn the book upside down, because that will shift your brain into a left-mode, and drawing is a right-mode activity.) Notice how the lines fit together and how they relate to the edges of the page. Notice also the "negative space" in the drawing — that is space outside of the actual figure. If you are unclear what I mean by this, hold your hand up to the light of a window and look at everything around it. This is what we call negative space.

As you begin to draw the picture, try not to think about what the lines are — just move from line to line, paying attention to space, relationships, and connections. Give yourself plenty of time to complete the drawing.

When you've finished, turn your drawing right side up. You'll be surprised at how good it is! Why does this work? Probably because the upside-down image throws your analytical, critical left brain for a loop, rendering it temporarily speechless while your right brain has fun with it.

Hot Tips for Creative Thinking

Remember Your Past Successes, Both the Humble and the Remarkable

If you were successful once (and we all have been at some time in our lives), you know you're a capable person who can do it again. Remind yourself of that when

Draw this figure using the instructions on the page to the left. (Resist turning the book upside down!)

you're working on a new challenge.

Believe This Can Be a Breakthrough Day

Approach your day with the belief that something *could* happen to change everything. That way if something really does come along, your eyes will already be open to it.

Exercise Your Creativity With Mental Games

Your brain, like any other part of your body, functions more smoothly if it's kept in tip-top condition. Here are some suggestions for doing that:

- Think of new uses for old things.
- Look at scenes from everyday life, and make up elaborate stories about the events that could have led to them.
- Do crossword puzzles and other word games.
- Invent metaphors you could use to describe something to somebody.
- Think of a lot of ways to say the same thing.
- Watch television with the sound off, and try to figure out what people are saying.

You can also try one of the many books of mental games on the market. (Several are listed in the "Recommended Resources" section at the end of this book.)

Remember That Failure Leads to Success

Many of the world's most famous scientists and inventors persevered through countless solutions that didn't work before finding one that did. Be willing to take the risk of being wrong in order to arrive at success.

Tips for Creativity Techniques

■ Remember your past successes, both the humble and the remarkable.

■ Believe this can be a breakthrough day.

■ Exercise your creativity with mental games.

■ Remember that failure leads to success.

■ Capture your dreams and fantasies.

■ Allow pleasure in your life.

■ Incorporate knowledge from other areas.

■ Look at the situation from all sides.

■ Clear your mind of assumptions.

■ Change your position occasionally.

Capture Your Dreams and Fantasies

Many times, dreams and fantasies are the product of your subconscious mind working on the solution to a problem. Give them credence, even if they seem far-fetched, because wild ideas can lead to innovative, even revolutionary, solutions.

Allow Pleasure in Your Life

Play! It lets the child in you come out and provides fresh insight. You'll also be more creative if your life is well balanced between work and play.

Incorporate Knowledge from Other Areas

When working with a challenging situation, look at other areas of your life and try to see similarities. Maybe something that works for one kind of problem can be adapted to the problem you're currently working on.

Look at the Situation from All Sides

Imagine yourself physically underneath looking up, from the top looking down, from the back and front, from inside looking out, and from the viewpoint of all of the parties involved. This allows you to see the situation from new windows and can provide just the insight you need for a creative solution.

Clear Your Mind of Assumptions

Assumptions can hide solutions. Consider this riddle: A police officer pulls over a car for speeding. Both cars stop. As the officer is walking up to the speeder's car, he notices six empty beer bottles on the floor behind the driver's seat.

"When did you drink those?" the officer asks.

New insights bring creativity into the real world.

Jason came from a family of engineers, and he expected to study engineering himself one day. He saw himself as a pragmatic person. Consequently, when he attended a class on creativity, he had trouble believing that he would ever use the techniques taught in the creativity class; he considered them to be somewhat ethereal.

Toward the end of the session, however, Jason experienced an "aha!" that provided everyone, even his teacher, with fresh inspiration.

"This class is liquid knowledge," he told her and the rest of the class. "You can't grab on to it, like you can math facts or grammar, but you can cup your hands and fill them up with it. Allow it to happen, and it will."

The instructor used Jason's metaphor of liquid knowledge and discussed the power of a liquid such as water, which will run through your fingers as softly as sand yet is powerful enough to carve the Grand Canyon.

A mind that's allowed to run its natural course can create equally magnificent things. That day Jason learned he must trust his innate creativity and give it permission to work, knowing that however far it wandered, it would eventually arrive at an answer. He also realized how valuable this creativity would be to him as an engineer. This realization made creativity applicable to real life and his world of pragmatism.

"Within the last hour," the driver replies.

When given the test for intoxication, the driver passes. The officer writes a ticket for speeding and lets the driver go. Why? Think about it for a while before checking the answer, which is at the end of this chapter.

Change Your Position Occasionally

If you're sitting at your desk, go outside and lie on the grass. Or if you're in the conference room at the office, switch seats with someone or stand up. Changing your position changes your view of things, and a physical shift might trigger a mental shift.

Answer

The beer is one of a growing number that are produced without alcohol. Did you assume the beer *had* to contain alcohol?

324 Thinking Logically, Thinking Creatively

I Know I Know

☑ Check the box if you understand the concept:

☐ I know I can think creatively.

☐ I know that creativity is a whole-brain process.

☐ I know the whole process of creating solutions, from laying the foundation to making them actually work:

1 _____   4 _____

2 _____   5 _____

3 _____

☐ I know I need to go through a period of doing nothing in order to start coming up with great ideas.

☐ I know how to use outcome thinking to attain my goals.

☐ I know how to think outside of my paradigms.

☐ I know that I can find solutions to all of the problems in my life.

12

Making That Quantum Learning Leap

Did you know . . .

that reviewing material greatly increases retention and understanding?

that putting closure on projects, classes, or stages of life is an important process for achieving success?

By now you know that everyone, including yourself, has enormous potential — the potential ability to be a genius. Your mind is virtually unlimited in its ability to learn — now and for the rest of your life. If you can accept this and find within yourself the motivation to pursue your highest goals, you will achieve a life of personal fulfillment and financial security.

Since review is an important tool for remembering and enhancing the material you learn, it's only fitting that we use this chapter to review and reflect upon the information in this book.

In Chapter 1, we began by defining Quantum Learning as "interactions that transform energy into radiance." For you, the learner, that means being able to feel within yourself the glow of well-being that occurs when all your energy is channeled toward successful solutions.

Most people will agree that Western society and the world as a whole are in a period of rapid change — both in technology and in collective consciousness. Along the path of progress are many global dilemmas to be resolved, and within each of us is the ability to reach mental breakthroughs that will lead to solutions.

Perhaps a reason for the disharmony and fragmentation in our world today is the phenomenon of increasing specialization. Each fragment of the population is intently focused on its own area of expertise and its own paradigms. Some say this phenomenon has been brought about — and made necessary — by the great volume of information available. With so much to know, a single individual can hope to know only a tiny part of a tiny part. While this is true, we now are finding it increasingly important to also understand the connectedness of everything.

René Descartes, the French philosopher and mathematician, said in 1619, "I begin to understand the foundations of a wonderful discovery . . . all the sciences are interconnected as by a chain; no one of them can be com-

With so much information available, a single individual can hope to know only a tiny part of a tiny part *and* it is increasingly important also to understand the connectedness of everything.

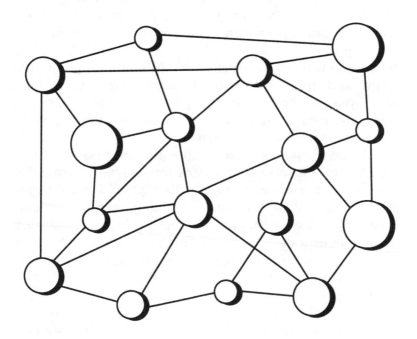

pletely grasped without taking in the whole ency-clopedia at once." (By *encyclopedia,* he didn't mean a set of books; he meant the totality of human knowledge.)

To become Quantum Learners, we must be able to process information in two ways: by assimilating chunks of material all at once, and by progressing from our understanding of the small units to knowing how these units operate on a large scale in conjunction with other factors. Usually, people find it easier to learn one way or the other (this is a function of learning style), but it's important to be able to do *both.*

The ability to enjoy learning and to learn with ease will lead you to exciting new areas of interest. And within each new area you'll find so many interesting avenues to explore that you'll be forever busy, forever learning, and forever intrigued with the intricacies of our world. As a bonus to this lifetime of exciting chal-lenge and the discovery of self-fulfillment, you'll become more and more valuable to your employers, your employees, and other people around you. Your success is more assured with each new piece of knowledge you have about the world and how it works.

If you doubt that you have the necessary mental equipment to become a Quantum Learner, remember that the brain you were born with is physiologically sim-ilar to those of people who are widely considered "gen-iuses," like Albert Einstein, Wolfgang Amadeus Mozart, and Leonardo da Vinci. This means your own brain is capable of greatness similar to the brains of those with advanced mental ability; you just have to learn how to guide it toward your own greatness.

As you discovered in Chapter 2, your ability to learn is determined by the amount of interactions among neu-rons in your brain. The more mental stimulation you receive, the more branching occurs within neurons, which increases the possibility of connections between neurons. So it's especially important to expose yourself to different and continually new forms of stimulation if you want to be a Quantum Learner. Exposure to var-

Like these renowned people, you have a brilliant mind and unlimited potential.

☆ Albert Einstein

☆ Mother Teresa

☆ Frank Lloyd Wright

☆ Buckminster Fuller

☆ Steven Spielberg

☆ Margaret Mead

☆ Your Name _____

ying kinds of activities and information is also important in balancing left- and right-brain capabilities.

This kind of exposure is a form of *active learning,*
which means taking responsibility for your own education and life by actively seeking the knowledge and
experiences you need. Active learning also means
actively seeking the *motivation* you need. Sometimes
you have to get and stay motivated by *creating interest*
in a subject — by somehow tying it into your everyday
life in a way that makes it easy to see benefit even when
others might find it obscure.

One way to create interest in a task is by telling
yourself "This is *it!*" As you learned in Chapter 3, if you
can take the most mundane task or intolerable situation
and give it 100 percent of your attention and enthusiasm, you'll easily become a master of "This is *it!*"
Transfer that enthusiasm to learning and practicing the
skills in this book, and you're well on your way to
becoming a Quantum Learner.

Your *ability* to use your learning skills is amplified
by a positive *attitude* — even when you feel you're sink-
ing in a bog of details and problems to solve, even when
you stumble repeatedly along the road to your goals.
You can just sit down in the muck and tell yourself
you'll never get anywhere — in which case you probably
won't — or you can remind yourself all along the way
that each little fumble is a learning experience that has
taught you something about how to reach that particular goal. And every little piece of knowledge will
eventually help you to reach your goal. Even better,
what you learned from each of those experiences can
help you in reaching other goals that you haven't even
set for yourself yet. In Chapter 4, we termed this "failure = feedback."

The way you talk to yourself is most important —
make your messages to yourself positive. Negativity
drains, while positivism energizes. Your home and work
environment are ideal places to start building pos-

Take responsibility for your education and life by actively seeking new knowledge and experiences.

- Take a course in something you never thought of taking before.

- Travel to new places.

- Do something that challenges you physically and emotionally:
  - rock climbing
  - white-water rafting
  - a long run
  - public speaking

- Model someone who is an expert in something that interests you.

- Subscribe to new publications.

- Experience a new cultural event.

- Develop a new hobby.

itivism. These "microenvironments" should be the strong foundations from which you venture out into the larger world, or "macroenvironment." Since it's so important that you face your challenges with a positive attitude, every detail of your personal work space should make a positive suggestion and make you feel comfortable and valuable. At SuperCamp, we take great care to build this kind of an environment for our students, and it is something you can build for yourself. Chapter 5 showed you lots of ways to do this.

Everyone has a personal learning style that can be used with great benefit in a variety of situations. It is important to be balanced in the way you perceive information as well as in how you order and process it. If you can decipher the learning styles of other people around you — like your spouse, children, your boss and employees, the knowledge can do wonders for your communication, rapport, and relationships with these people.

Skills Are for Using

The tools presented in this book are simply that — tools. Like any other set of tools, they don't do anything by themselves; you have to *use* them. You could liken them to the tools in your garage or workshop. Some are simple and their benefit is instantly available, like that of a screwdriver. Others, like a jigsaw perhaps, take some real concentration and practice before you become proficient with them. In the reading chapter, for instance, learning to use your finger is like learning to use a screwdriver. Warp reading, on the other hand, is more comparable to using a jigsaw.

If you know how to drive a car with a manual transmission, you probably remember how awkward it felt when you were learning how to do it. All of your limbs seemed to flail wildly in different directions, and coordinating all the movements took so much concentration that you couldn't possibly do anything else at the same

Quantum Learners learn with ease by following these guidelines.

Preview

Read ahead, preview material the night before, and look over notes before your class or presentation.

"This Is *It*!"

Make the most of every moment, make subjects interesting, and be creative.

Study Area

Study at a regular place and time. Practice good posture and use good lighting.

Play Music

Baroque music helps you learn more by relaxing your mind and keeping you alert.

Take Breaks

Every 30 minutes, take a short 5-minute break. Learning is best just before and after a break.

Plan Ahead

Use your calendar to prepare for a test or presentation. You will reduce stress and enhance recall.

Stand and Sit Tall

When entering a room, walk tall to feel confident. Sit tall in your chair to feel interested and alert.

Failure Is Feedback

Feedback is information needed to be successful and provides direction.

Attitude

We can accomplish more than we ever dreamed possible, when we put our minds to it!

time, like talk to someone in the passenger seat. And yet now you can do it all without even thinking. You may even have enough skill to talk on your cellular phone, drink coffee, and downshift while turning a corner — all at the same time.

You can become proficient at the skills in this book in the same way that repetition has made driving a manual transmission feel like second nature to you.

Hot Tips

Here are the hottest tips from each chapter to help you on your quest for Quantum Learning.

Find a Benefit in Everything You Do

Make a game of it, if necessary.

Give Yourself Positive Pats on the Back

Talk about yourself in a positive manner, and avoid people who give you needlessly negative feedback. Reframe negative feedback in the most positive way you can. For instance, rather than taking a negative comment personally, tell yourself, "Gee, he must be having a really bad day to say something like that to me." Believe you can reach your goals, for if you believe, you will succeed.

Create a Safety Zone for Yourself . . .

in your home, and gradually expand it to include your office, the great outdoors, the lecture hall, social situations, and so on. Take steps outside your safety zone, for this is what forces it to expand. Step back inside to assimilate new information and consolidate your energy.

Skills are tools to be used. With concentration and practice, you will become proficient with them.

*L*ike any other set of tools, they don't do anything by themselves —

you have to use them.

Be Conscious of Your Learning Style . . .

in every situation. Make adjustments to help yourself absorb input, and help others to absorb *your* input.

Use One or Both of the Note-Taking Methods . . .

you learned (Mind Mapping and Notes:TM) in as many situations as you can. They can be adapted for most any reason you find to put pen to paper. These are "jigsaw" skills; you will become more and more comfortable with them with practice, and you will find more and more uses for them.

Think of Writing as a Fun Activity . . .

in which every individual has unique talent, and remember that you have many ways of overcoming writer's block *and* the ability to write creatively.

Be Conscious of All the Different Reading Speeds Available to You . . .

and vary your speed according to the task at hand. Practice warp reading often, for this is another "jigsaw" skill that takes concentration and repeated use before proficiency is achieved.

Tell Yourself There's an Opportunity to Think Creatively in Every Situation . . .

then make the effort to do it! This may feel like a strain at first, but will become more and more natural the more you do it. Eventually, people will start referring to you as a "creative person" and these references alone will reinforce your self-image, so you'll become even more creative.

To Increase Your Memory Ability, Remember to Remember, and —

Tips for Quantum Learning

- Find a benefit.

- Give yourself positive pats.

- Create a safe place for working.

- Be conscious of your learning style.

- Practice Notes:TM and Mind Mapping.

- Think of writing as fun.

- Be aware of available reading speeds.

- Think creatively in all situations.

- Remember to remember.

Remember to Use Your Skills

Most important, learning should be a positive experience. By thinking positively and making the practical skills your own, you're making a mental shift that will enable you to help change the world. Fill yourself with as much light as possible. And let your light shine.

Remember to use your skills

&

remember to have fun.

And when you have finally reached your goal . . .

Recommended Resources

Books

Note-Taking

Buzan, Tony. *Use Both Sides of Your Brain, 3rd ed.*
New York: Penguin Books, 1989.

Margulies, Nancy. *Mapping Inner Space.* Tucson:
Zephyr Press, 1991.

Wycoff, Joyce. *Mindmapping.* New York: The Berkley
Publishing Group, 1991.

Reading

Agardy, Franklin J. *How to Read Faster and Better.*
New York: Simon & Schuster, 1981.

Saperstein, Rose, and James Joseph. *Read Your Way to
the Top with the Guide.* Seattle: Bluechip Publishers,
1987.

Writing

Caplan, Rebekah. *Writers in Training.* Palo Alto, Calif.:
Dale Seymour Publications, 1982.

Elbow, Peter. *Writing Without Teachers.* New York:
Oxford University Press, 1973.

Rico, Gabriele Lusser. *Writing the Natural Way*. Los Angeles: Jeremy P. Tarcher, 1983. Distributed by St. Martin's Press.

Creativity

deBono, Edward. *Lateral Thinking, Creativity Step by Step*. New York: Harper & Row, 1973.

Edwards, Betty. *Drawing on the Right Side of the Brain*. Los Angeles: Jeremy P. Tarcher, 1979.

Harman, Willis, and Howard Rheingold. *Higher Creativity: Liberating the Unconscious for Breakthrough Insights*. Los Angeles: Jeremy P. Tarcher, 1984. Distributed by St. Martin's Press.

Sinetar, Marsha. *Developing a 21st Century Mind*. New York: Villard Books, 1991.

Learning Styles

Armstrong, Thomas. *In Their Own Way*. Los Angeles: Jeremy P. Tarcher, 1987.

Butler, Kathleen A., Ph.D. *It's All in Your Mind: A Student's Guide to Learning Style*. Columbia, Conn.: The Learner's Dimension, 1988.

Gregorc, Anthony. *An Adult's Guide to Style*. Maynard, Mass: Gabriel Systems, 1982.

Learning

Armstrong, Thomas. *Awakening Your Child's Natural Genius*. Los Angeles: Jeremy P. Tarcher, 1991.

Dickinson, Dee. *Creating the Future, Perspectives on Educational Change.* Aston Clinton, Bucks: Accelerated Learning Systems Ltd., 1991.

Gardner, Howard. *Frames of Mind: The Theory of Multiple Intelligences.* London: Fontana Press, 1993, n.e..

Grinder, Michael. *Righting the Educational Conveyer Belt.* Portland, Ore.: Metamorphous Press, 1991.

Kiyosaki, Robert. *If You Want to Be Rich & Happy, Don't Go to School?* San Diego: The Excellerated Learning Company, 1991.

Kline, Peter. *The Everyday Genius.* Arlington, Va.: Great Ocean Publishers, 1988.

Rose, Colin. *Accelerated Learning.* Topaz Publishing, 1985.

The Brain and Our Potential

Bandler, Richard. *Using Your Brain for a Change.* Moab, Utah: Real People Press, 1985.

Buzan, Tony. *Make the Most of Your Mind.* London: Pan Books, 1988, n.e..

Diamond, Marian Cleeves. *Enriching Heredity.* New York: The Free Press, A Division of Macmillan, Inc., 1988.

Herrmann, Ned. *The Creative Brain.* Lake Lure, N.C.: Brain Books, 1988.

MacLean, Paul. *The Triune Brain in Evolution.* New York: Plenum, 1990.

Pearce, Joseph Chilton. *Magical Child.* New York: E.P. Dutton, 1977.

Robbins, Anthony. *Awaken the Giant Within.* London: Simon & Schuster, 1992.

Robbins, Anthony. *Unlimited Power.* London: Simon & Schuster, 1989.

Mental Games

Gardner, Martin. *aha! Insight.* New York: Scientific American/W.H. Freeman and Company, 1978.

Raudsepp, Eugene. *Creative Growth Games.* New York: The Putnam Publishing Group, 1977.

Raudsepp, Eugene. *More Creative Growth Games.* New York: Perigee Books, 1980.

Wujec, Tom. *Pumping Ions.* New York: Doubleday & Co., 1988.

Study Skills

Gall, Meredith. *Study for Success.* Eugene, Ore.: M. Damien Publishers, 1985.

Jensen, Eric. *Student Success Secrets.* New York: Barron's Educational Series, 1989.

Ohme, Herman. *Learn How to Learn.* Palo Alto, Calif.: California Education Plan, 1989.

Teaching and Presenting

Ailes, Roger. *You Are the Message.* Homewood, Ill.: Dow Jones-Irwin, 1988.

Dhority, Lynn. *The ACT Approach: The Artful Use of Suggestion for Integrative Learning.* Bremen, Germany: PLS Verlag, 1991.

Gelb, Michael J. *Present Yourself.* Rolling Hills Estates, Calif.: Jalmar Press, 1988.

Jensen, Eric. *Superteaching.* Dubuque, Iowa: Kendall Hunt Publishing Company, 1988.

Peoples, David A. *Presentations Plus.* New York: John Wiley & Sons, 1988.

Philosophy

Heider, John. *Tao of Leadership.* Atlanta, Ga.: Humanics, Ltd., 1984.

Huang, Chungliang Al. *Embrace Tiger, Return to Mountain,* 2nd ed. Berkeley, Calif.: Celestial Arts, 1987.

Huang, Chungliang Al. *Quantum Soup.* New York: Celestial Arts, 1991.

Audio and Videotapes

Allen, Rich. *How to Build a Winning Attitude*. Oceanside, Calif.: Learning Forum Success Products, 1988. Videotape.

Bohannon, Bonnie. *Be a Confident Math Solver*. Oceanside, Calif.: Learning Forum Success Products, 1988. Videotape.

Bornstein, Scott. *How to Increase Your Memory 10 Times*. Oceanside, Calif.: Learning Forum Success Products, 1988. Videotape.

Brown, Linda. *How to Understand and Be Understood*. Oceanside, Calif.: Learning Forum Success Products, 1988. Videotape.

Carr, Michael. *Success Through Writing*. Oceanside, Calif. : Learning Forum Success Products, 1988. Videotape.

DePorter, Bobbi. *Unleashing the Genius in You with Quantum Learning*. Oceanside, Calif.: Learning Forum Success Products, 1989. Audiotape.

Edmondson, Amy. *Take the Mystery Out of Algebra*. Oceanside, Calif.: Learning Forum Success Products, 1988. Videotape.

Jensen, Eric. *"Map" Your Way to Better Grades*. Oceanside, Calif.: Learning Forum Success Products, 1988. Videotape.

Neale, Kate. *Take Quantum Leaps in Your Reading Speed*. Oceanside, Calif.: Learning Forum Success Products, 1988. Videotape.

Snyder, Steve. *Alpha Learning*. Oceanside, Calif.: Learning forum Success Products, 1988. Audiotape.

For information about SuperCamp and Learning Forum Success Products contact:

Learning Forum
SuperCamp
1725 South Hill Street
Oceanside, CA 92054–5319
USA
Tel: (619) 722 0072.

Index

Abstract random thinkers,
124, 132-134,
138-139
Abstract sequential thinkers,
124, 134-136, 140
Accelerated learning, 14, 16,
72
Acronyms, use of in memory,
236-237
Active learning, 52, 54-55,
332
Active reading, 264
Age:
    effect on ability to learn,
      84
    effect on memory,
      208-210
Analytical thinking, 298-299
Association:
    in clustering, 182, 184
    importance in memory,
      208, 213-214,
      216-219, 222-230,
      234
    importance in
    note-taking,
      170
Association method for
    memory, 216-218
Attitude, 335
    See also Positive attitude
Auditory learners, 112-123,
140
Benefits, finding, 46-62, 336
    creating interest, 48,
      50-53, 266, 332
    "this is it!," 58-62, 332,
      335
    personal power, 50,
      56-57, 78
Bornstein, Scott, 232
Brain:
    dominance, 111, 124-141
    emotional-cognitive
      function of, 28, 32-33
    exercising, 320

left side of the, 26, 36-40, 74,
    178-179, 186,
    299-300, 306, 318,
    332
limbic system, 26-30, 34,
    40
mammalian, 26-29, 34
neocortex, 26-30, 34, 80
physiology of the, 26-40,
    80, 330
reptile, 26-29, 34
right side of the, 36-40, 74,
    178-180, 186,
    299-300, 306, 318,
    332
sensory motor function of,
    28-29, 32
storage of information in,
    150-51, 154, 212
thought patterns of, 155,
    180-182
triune theory of, 16,
    26-29
whole-, 26, 40,
    152-153, 178-179
Brainstorming, 160, 302,
    310-317
Breaks:
    as aid to memory, 242
    music for, 74
    importance of taking,
      84, 86, 335
Burklyn Business School,
    11-12
Buzan, Tony, 152
California Writing Project,
    194-195
Canfield, Jack, 24
Caplan, Rebekah, 190
Celebration as a reward, 56,
    58-59, 62, 341
Clustering, 180-86, 192, 194,
    312
Comfort zone:
    expanding 60, 68-69
    stepping out of, 92, 171